THE S

Piddlehinton

C000182207

DORSET BOOKS

CONTENTS

LIST OF SUBSCRIBERS

Maureen A. Adams (née Holbrook), *2317 Parliament Avenue, Regina, Saskatchewan, Canada*

Mrs Jacqueline Alford, *16 Victoria Road, Dorchester*

Neville and Jean Anderson, *The Thimble Inn, Piddlehinton* (from 1970 to 1985)

Sheila Austin, *3 Quarrs Close, North Bowood, Bridport*

Mr Howard G. Baker, *72 Cambridge Road, Dorchester*

Edward P. Baker, *Robinswood, Dewlish, Dorchester*

Jack C. W. Baker, *1 Brutus Close, Dorchester*

Mrs N. Baker, *3 Nutts End, Piddletrenthide*

Mrs Ione Banner, *Kiddlescombe, Piddletrenthide*

Miss Jan C. Barclay, *59 Cynthia Road, Parkstone, Poole*

Mrs L. C. Barnes, *1 Beech Road, Puddletown*

Mr A. W. Barrett, *58 Mellstock Avenue, Dorchester*

Miss D. E. R. Barrett, *4 Minerva Close, Dorchester*

Joy Barrett, *128 Coburg Road, Dorchester*

C. M. M. Barrow, *Mornewood Cottage, Piddlehinton*

John R. Bartlett, *30 Portalfield, Stalham, Norfolk*

Peter A. Bartlett, *Pendomer, 13 King Creek Road, Wauchope, New South Wales, Australia*

A. R. Batchelor, *269 High Street, Epping, Essex*

Mr Marcus Batten, *2 The Green, Puddletown, Dorchester*

Jos and Sue Belgrave, *Storrington, West Sussex*

Robert and Susan Belgrave, *West Lodge, Piddlehinton*

R. R. D. Belgrave, *North Kilworth, Leicestershire*

Denise and Brian Bere, *1 The Willows, Cheselbourne, Nr Dorchester*

B. H. Blackwell Ltd, *Hythe Bridge Street, Oxford*

Mr J. Edward Boardman, *29 Wellfields Drive, Bridport*

Mr K. Boardman, *Barn Cottage, 17A North Street, Charminster, Dorchester*

Mrs Margaret Boardman (née Jeanes), *29 Wellfields Drive, Bridport*

John and Anne Bouffler, *Meadow Cottage, Puddletown*

S. G. Brackstone, *Riverway, White Lackington, Piddletrenthide*

Dulcie and Mike Brian, *Orchardlands, Hilton, Blandford*

Mr H. Broad, *7 Alderley Road, Northbourne, Bournemouth*

Mrs H. M. Brockway, *12 Rectory Road, Piddlehinton*

Mrs G. E. Brook, *18 Yester Road, Chislehurst, Kent*

R. A. and S. H. Brookfield, *16 Park Lane, Cannington, Bridgwater, Somerset*

Jonathan Buchan, *Jersey Farmhouse, Piddletrenthide*

Robert and Pat Buchan, *Piddlehinton Post Office, 2A Rectory Road, Piddlehinton*

Elizabeth Caffin, *Auckland, New Zealand*

Mrs P. M. Caldwell, *Whetstones, 2A High Street, Piddlehinton*

Mrs Elizabeth Carter, *School House, Kelly College, Tavistock, Devon*

Mrs William L. Cary, *1120 Fifth Avenue, New York, USA*

Mr and Mrs J. F. Chapman, *19 Paynes Close, Piddlehinton*

S. B. Chapman, *Hope House, Winterbourne Zelston, Blandford*

Ben Cheeseman, *22 London Close, Piddlehinton*

Mr E. Cheeseman, *28 Paddington Grove, Bournemouth*

Ernest D. Cheeseman, *The Beacon, Osmington Mills, Weymouth*

The Christophers Family, *Ivy Cottage, 2 High Street, Piddlehinton*

Mrs J. Clare (née Hawkins), *The Jays, Blagdon Close, Martinstown*

Lyn Cole, *46 Fourgates Road, Dorchester*

Dr S. G. Corbin, *64 Pound Lane, Poole*

David Cosh, *15 Hutchins Close, Castle Park, Dorchester*

Mr Edward Cosh, *2 Bold Acre, Alton Pancras, Dorchester*

Mr A. C. E. Coton, MCFA, MRSH, *The Pantiles, 2 Heanor Close, Winton, Bournemouth*

Alfred J. Coulthard, *Colescote, Piddletrenthide*

Eric Cox, *2 St Catherines Way, Down End, Fareham, Hampshire*

Mr and Mrs F. W. Crisp, *2 Canon Close, Rochester, Kent*

Barry Cuff, *27 Badgers Way, Sturminster Newton*

Kathleen Curzon, *23 Paynes Close, Piddlehinton*

Mr & Mrs Roy Damen, *11 High Street, Piddlehinton*

Mrs M. R. Dangerfield, *Beechmead, Alton Pancras, Dorchester*

Neville Dear, *4 Merriefield Close, Broadstone, Poole*

Elizabeth Deasy, *Kingston Cottage, Long Bredy, Dorchester*

J. and J. M. Deavin, *6 Whites Close, Piddlehinton*

John W. A. Diggens, *8 High Street, Piddlehinton*

Cleveland and Phyllis Dodge, *Pownal, Vermont, USA*

Mr Shaun Doel, *28B Little London, Heytesbury, Warminster, Wiltshire*

Dorset Natural History and Archaeological Society, *Dorset County Museum, Dorchester*

Sir Robert and Lady Drew, *Sydney, Australia*

Mrs Tracy E. Dunne, *40, Egmont Road, Hamworthy, Poole*

Margie Edwards, *Mullets, Piddletrenthide*

Maurice Edwards, *Mullets, Piddletrenthide*

R. J. A. Edwards. *Holcombe Dairy House, Alton Pancras, Dorchester*

Mike Ellery, *58 Cromwell Road, Weymouth*

Norman and Gay Elliot, *The Old School House, Rectory Road, Piddlehinton*

Sue and David Elliot, *The Forge, 103 The Causeway, Burwell, Cambridge*

Eton College, *Eton, Windsor, Berkshire*

Ian Everitt, *11 Whites Close, Piddlehinton*

Ada May Farmer (née Riggs), *8 Ethel Brooks House, Eghinton Road, Plumstead, London*

Mr C. Forgeard, *299 Sopwith Crescent, Merley, Wimborne*

Stephen Fox, *The Poachers Inn, Piddletrenthide*

Mr R. France, *57 Mount Road, Kinson, Bournemouth*

Mr & Mrs J. W. L. French, *Venta Silurum, Waterston, Piddlehinton*

N. D. Frisby, *Broadmayne, Dorchester*

Eveline Gabe, *8 Bayeux Court, Dorchester*

Mrs S. B. Gane, *The Rock, 18 The Green, Stoford, Yeovil, Somerset*

David and Louise Garratt, *18 Paynes Close, Piddlehinton*

Mr Clive Gerrard, *23 Edward Road, Dorchester*

Mrs Winifred Gerrard, *19 London Close, Piddlehinton*

Mr N. E. M. Giles, *12 Derby Street, Weymouth*

Mrs Lilian Gillingham, *23 Balfour Road, Bournemouth*

Mr D. C. and Mrs M. Goddard, *The Courtyard, Long Burton, Sherborne*

Mr Frank Godman, *Hillbarn Cottage, Wolfeton Farm, Charminster, Dorchester*

Sarah Goodbody (née Lovelace), *Brimstone Cottage, Holworth, Dorchester*

Chris Gouldsbury, *Laneast, 1 Whites Close, Piddlehinton*

Peter Gregory, *9 Paynes Close, Piddlehinton*

Wendy Gregory, *13 Capella Road, Northwood, Middlesex*

Mrs J. M. Griffiths, *The Garden Cottage, Rectory Road, Piddlehinton*

Mrs Angela Grist, *Rusper House, Piddlehinton*

Mrs Margaret E. Gulliford, *Kenamar, Ridge Farm, Higher Waterston, Dorchester*

Mrs Winifred Hadsel, *106 White Street, Lexington, Virginia, USA*

T. M. Haggett, *Fox Hollow, 5 Whites Cottage, Piddlehinton*

David Hames, *99 North Street, Bere Regis, Wareham*

Mr and Mrs Charles Hammick, *Higher Waterston Farm*

V. P. and R. Hamshaw, *Robin Hill, Bradford Peverell, Dorchester*

Mrs E. G. R. Hanbury, *Sparrows Thatch, 3 London Row, Piddlehinton*

Mrs Janet Ann Hansford (née Rose), *18 London Close, Piddlehinton*
Mr and Mrs N. J. G. Harland, *Quinces, London Row, Piddlehinton*
J. W. Harper, *3 High Street, Piddlehinton*
R. W. Harper, *3 High Street, Piddlehinton*
Mrs Annette Harpur (née Tory), *Llanbrynean, Llanfrynach, Brecon, Powys*
Mrs G. E. Hatcher, *7 Jacobs Ladder, Child Okeford, Blandford*
Mrs P. Hatfield, *College Library, Eton College*
Mrs Nora Head, *5 The Folly, Cerne Abbas, Dorchester*
A. C. B. Helps, *Bridle Gates, Hogshill Lane, Cobham, Surrey*
Vera Hewitt (née Vincent), *18 Warwick Avenue, Coventry*
Mr David Holland, *Puddle Farm, Dales Corner, Piddlehinton*
Brian Holtham, *Willoughby House, Puddletown*
Mr Frank Hornyak, *9 High Street, Piddlehinton*
Everett J. House, *116 Bodliham, Salisbury, Wiltshire*
A. and R. Howard, *4 Church Hill, Piddlehinton*
Mrs Sally Howard-Tripp (née Tory), *Kingsmead, Piddletrenthide*
Mr and Mrs Alfred H. Howell, *4602 Palisade Avenue, Bronx, New York, USA*
Mrs N. P. Hughes, *Yondover Farmhouse, Loders, Bridport*
John and Rosemary Jackson, *Casterbridge, 64 Fairfield Road, Widnes, Cheshire*
Mr Terry Jeanes, *9 London Close, Piddlehinton*
Helen Kavanagh, *93 Olive Road, Coxford, Southampton*
Mr and Mrs Hugh Kelsey, *Whites Dairy House, Piddlehinton*
D. H. Kenchington (in memory of the late Kathleen P. Kenchington), *16 Wellstead Road, Northmoor Park, Wareham*
Mrs Edith Lamb, *3 Caesar Green, Castle Park, Dorchester*
Lt Cdr and Mrs R. Lamb, *Longpuddle, 4 High Street, Piddlehinton*
Mary and Michael Lanfranchi, *North Kilworth, Leicestershire*
Mrs Joan Lanham, *43 Rectory Road, Dickleburgh, Diss, Norfolk*
Pamela Legg (née Cosh), *1 Paynes Close, Piddlehinton*
Hilary Letham, RMN, *72 High Bank Park, Lochgilphead, Argyll*
Mrs G. L. Light, *Monks Cottage, 70 South Court Avenue, Dorchester*
Mrs P. M. Lockyer, *69 Celtic Crescent, Dorchester*
Sir Donald and Lady Logan, *6 Thurloe Street, London*
Mrs Fay Lord, *Pydel Nook, Paynes Close, Piddlehinton*
Ian Donald Lord, *3 Swanscombe Place, Up Hatherley, Cheltenham, Gloucestershire*
Ronald Colin Lord, *25 St Pauls Close, Four Pools, Evesham, Worcestershire*
R. Machin, *The Grey Cottage, Askerswell, Dorset*
Mrs Dorothy MacMahon, *20 Paynes Close, Piddlehinton*
MacMahon, *Lambert Cottage, White Lackington, Piddletrenthide*
Miss Marion Makinson, *41 Casterbridge Road, Dorchester*
Mrs E. A. Mapletoft, (née Dyke), *Spridlington Manor Farm, Spridlington, Lincolnshire*
Carly Marrin, *Grange Cottage, Oborne, Sherborne*
Cecilia Marrin, *Grange Cottage, Oborne, Sherborne*
Dr Charles Marrin, *Hartland, Vermont, USA*
Jane Marrin, *58 Lansdowne Road, London*
John Marrin, *27a Lansdowne Crescent, London*
A. P. Mayne, *West House, Piddletrenthide*
K. M. Mayo, *14 Church Acre, Dorchester*
Mr and Mrs L. J. Mayo, *Cokers Frome Farm, Dorchester*
Mr and Mrs R. Mayo, *Higher Farm, Rodden, Weymouth*
Ross and Loraine McClean, *The Old Stables, High Street, Piddlehinton*
Mrs J. McFadden, *Harmony House, 34 Warnford Road, Boscombe East, Bournemouth*

D. McIntyre, *14 Southville Road, Southbourne, Bournemouth*
Mrs S. J. McSwiggan, *2 Norman Avenue, Branksome, Poole*
Heather Mentern (née Read), *3 Ash Hill, Stratton (formerly Piddlehinton), Nr Dorchester*
R. P. and E. G. Mew, *Greyholme, 7 Whites Close, Piddlehinton*
Simon, Alice and Jack Moore, *16 Paynes Close, Piddlehinton*
Michael and Jo Moore, *Poppies, 32 Paynes Close, Piddlehinton*
Audrey Moreton (a Way descendant), *22 Imber Road, Winnall, Winchester, Hampshire*
Mrs A. E. Neades, *Westward, White Lackington, Piddletrenthide*
David and Jean Newsom, *Washington DC, USA*
Mrs A. Louise Nordin, *405 Heritage House, 8315–105 Street, Edmonton, Alberta, Canada*
Mr W. Northover, *Greenacres, Spetisbury, Nr Blandford*
Mr and Mrs O. B. N. Paine, *Muston Manor, Piddlehinton*
Rev. Derek Parry, *The Vicarage, Piddletrenthide*
Mrs Y. Payne, *Maplemead, Briantspuddle, Dorchester*
W. R. Pearce, *Le Domaine, Piddletrenthide*
Nigel and Kristina Pearce-Buckley, *Manor Bungalow, Piddletrenthide*
Mr Jack Pearson, *Manor Cottage, Lower Waterston, Dorchester*
Roger Peers, *20 Frome Terrace, Dorchester*
David Pickering Pick, *1 Christ Church Villas, Malvern Road, Cheltenham, Gloucestershire*
Muriel Pike, *Abbot's Ford, Piddletrenthide*
The Earl of Portarlington, *Sydney, Australia*
Mr and Mrs A. G. Read, *Wyne Bourne, Dales Corner, Piddlehinton*
Jean and Norman Reddaway, *51 Carlton Hill, London*
Mr and Mrs J. F. Reeby, *The Spa House, Nottington, Weymouth*
P. and M. F. Robson, *26 Paynes Close, Piddlehinton*
Nora Roper and Edward Roper, *64 Weatherbury Way, Manor Park, Dorchester*
Mary and Bernard Roughton, *2 Rectory Road, Piddlehinton*
Mrs May Rowlands, *London, Ontario, Canada*
B. K. Roy, *Piddletrenthide*
Miss J. A. W. Roy, *Altona, Grove Road, Wickhambreaux, Canterbury*
Mrs Donna Russell, *9 Robin Close, Midsomer Norton, Bath, Avon*
Ken Russell, *Kenwyn, 71 Meadow View, Charminster, Dorset*
St Mary's C E Middle School, *Puddletown*
Mrs J. Samways, *20 St Martins Field, Martinstown, Dorchester*
Mrs D. Sawyer, *12 High Street, Piddlehinton*
Peter John Sawyer, *1 Bourne Drove, Dale's Corner, Piddlehinton*
Mr and Mrs Ian Scott, *15 Briar Walk, London SW15*
Mrs Jean Shave, *1 Gypsy Row, Piddletrenthide*
Mr Walter George Sims, *c/o 25 Thornham Road, Ashley, New Milton, Hampshire*
Mr and Mrs K. D. J. Slowe and Family, *The Coach House, Piddlehinton*
Naomi Smeeth, *21 London Close, Piddlehinton*
Tony Smeeth, *6811 Wooslawn Avenue NE, #33, Seattle, Washington, USA*
Miss Barbara Smith, *2 Brymer Road, Puddletown*
Mr Kenneth Spiller, *Hill Dairy, Piddlehinton*
Miss Lois Spiller, *Hill Dairy, Piddlehinton*
Mr Richard Spiller, *Hill Dairy, Piddlehinton*
Mrs Tessa Spiller, *Hill Dairy, Piddlehinton*
Ivor and Rose Marie Sprackling, *8 Trusthams, Broadwindsor, Beaminster*
R. Staniforth, *26 Winslow Road, Preston, Weymouth*
Mr and Mrs D. B. Stanton, *7 Rectory Road, Piddlehinton*
M. J. Steele, *7 Alexandra Road, Dorchester*
Mrs F. M. Stuart-Williams, *The Hoppits, 17 Church End, Braughing, Nr Ware, Hertfordshire*

Mrs R. A. Suter, *c/o Hawthorn Cottage, Rectory Road, Piddlehinton*

Rosemarie Suter (née Lovelace), *c/o Brimstone Cottage, Holworth, Dorchester*

Brian and Coleen Swindell, *Little Beck, Whites Close, Piddlehinton*

Mrs N. R. Swyer, *18 Weld Court, West Walks Road, Dorchester*

Sir Gordon and Lady Tait, *Auckland, New Zealand*

Mr and Mrs T. Teichroew, *10118 Radford Avenue NW, Seattle, Washington, USA*

Percy and Dorothy Teversham, *Springdale, Cheselbourne, Nr Dorchester (Married in Piddlehinton Church, 23.12.44)*

Mrs Jane Thomas (née Tory), *Woodlands, Higher Brockhampton, Dorchester*

Mr W. A. Thomas, *5 Homechester House, Dorchester*

Mr David Thompson and Mrs Mary Thompson, *17 Paynes Close, Piddlehinton*

B. Tilbrook, *2 Redlands, Piddletrenthide*

Brian M. Till, *The Granary, Piddletrenthide*

Mrs Elsie G. Toms, *647 Dorchester Road, Broadwey, Weymouth*

J. P. L. Tory, *Home Farm, Bryanston, Blandford*

Mrs M. E. Tory, *Five Bells House, Piddletrenthide*

Mrs P Tory-Stehr, MBE, *35a South Street, Dorchester*

C. A. E. Treasure, *7 Monmouth Road, Wareham*

Mrs B. Trim, *17 Avebury Avenue, Bournemouth*

Paul Tyler, *Hill House, Notton, Dorchester*

Robert Vickery, *Lea Farm Cottage, Waterston, Dorchester*

William Vickery, *Lea Farm Cottage, Waterston, Dorchester*

W. J. Vickery, *Lea Farm, Waterston, Dorchester*

Gaius Vincent, *Muston Farm, Piddlehinton*

Sally Vincent, *Broadwey, Weymouth*

Christopher R. J. Viner, *Elmsbrook, West Street, Winterbourne Kingston, Blandford*

Miss P. Voss, *26 Alington Road, Dorchester*

Claire Waddy, *West Cottage, Piddletrenthide*

Gerald Walbrin, *1 Little Wrackleford Cottage, Wrackleford, Dorchester*

Mrs Linda Walbrin (née Damen), *2 Paynes Close, Piddlehinton*

M. J. Warden, *40 Cornwall Road, Dorchester*

Helen Wardlaw, *4 Whites Close, Piddlehinton*

Jessica Wardlaw, *4 Whites Close, Piddlehinton*

Nicholas Wardlaw, *4 Whites Close, Piddlehinton*

E. Warwick, *101 Alexandria Road, Parkstone, Poole*

Mr Christopher Way, *9 Whites Close, Piddlehinton*

Mrs Ivy Way, *10 Beech Road, Puddletown, Dorchester*

Reginald Wickett, *67 Conway Road, Cardiff, Wales*

K. P. Wightman, *19A Hamlyn Road, Glastonbury, Somerset*

T. R. Wightman, *32 St Catherine's Crescent, Sherborne*

Mrs Mark Williams (née Churchill), *5 Winters Lane, Portesham, Near Weymouth*

Jim Wills, *18 Downfield, Winterborne Stickland, Blandford Forum*

Thelma B. Wills, *21 Mountain Ash Road, Dorchester*

Mrs J. I. Winter, *102 Brunel Road, Old Redbridge, Southampton*

Audrey Wirdnam, *Beechcote, 1 The Green, Tolpuddle*

Peter Woods, *Riverhill House, 7 Easts Hill, Charminster*

Mary and Tony Wright, *Purbeck Close, Weymouth*

Robert R. Wright, *Waterways, Piddletrenthide*

Dr and Mrs Wylie, *Sharon, Connecticut, USA*

Mrs Laura Yeatman-Smith, *Blysmere, 10 Whites Close, Piddlehinton*

First published 1990
Copyright © Piddlehinton Village Hall Sub-committee 1990

British Library Cataloguing-in-Publication Data
The story of Piddlehinton.
 1. Dorset. Piddlehinton. Social life history
 942.3'31

ISBN 1–871164–07–9

Phototypeset by Vine & Gorfin Ltd
Printed and bound in Great Britain by Printline

DORSET BOOKS   An imprint of Wheaton Publishers Ltd.
A Member of Maxwell Communication Corporation plc

Wheaton Publishers Ltd   Hennock Road, Marsh Barton, Exeter, Devon EX2 8RP Tel: 0392 74121; Telex 42794 (WHEATN G)

SALES   Direct sales enquiries to Dorset Books at the address above.

ACKNOWLEDGEMENTS   We acknowledge our gratitude to the following: The Dorset Natural History and Archaelogical Society, especially Roger Peers, Curator, and Judy Morris (photographs and extracts from Dorset County Chronicle); The Provost and Fellows of Eton College, especially Mrs Hatfield, archivist (photograph on p. 12 and excerpts from their archives); The Royal Commission on the Historical Monuments of England (1867 plan of church); Hanford Farms Ltd; The National Society, Church House, Westminster (details of nineteenth-century schooling); Messrs Hall & Woodhouse, Blandford (photograph and details of the New Inn); Dorset Police, especially P.C. N. Frisby (extract from *The Dorset Constabulary*); Stone's Monumental Masons, Weymouth and Dorchester (information about War Memorial); *The Piddle Valley Book of Country Life*, Dorset County Record Office; Dorset County Reference Library, Dorchester; Dorset County Library; Dorset Military Museum; The Lock Collection, at Dorset County Library (for photographs and paintings by Mary and Kate Hardy); Robert Machin, University of Bristol. We are also very grateful to everyone who shared their knowledge of Piddlehinton with us and to the many who contributed photographs, including: Nellie Baker, Nora Barnes, Peter Bartlett, Alfred Batchelor, Dawn Batten (née Way), Robert Belgrave, Dickie and Di Bird, Margaret Boardman (née Jeanes), Ben Cheeseman, John Churchill, Robert Coombs, Joyce Clare (née Hawkins), Alfred Coulthard, Wyn Gerrard (née Riggs), Sarah Goodbody (née Lovelace), Nancy Green, Jack Gregory, John Gregory, the late Emily Gregory, Pat Hansford, Mrs N. A. Head, Vera Hewitt (née Vincent), Jim Hooper, Harry Hounsell, Joan Lanham (née Croft), Pam Legg (née Cosh), Rosmond Lester (née Green), Margaret Lister-Kaye, Geoff and Fay Lord (née Jeanes), Charles Mayo, Robert and Ann Mayo, Barry and Paddy Paine, Rev. Derek Parry, Muriel Pike, Iris Rose (née Reid), Nora Roper (née Groves), May Rowlands, Tony Smeeth, Laura Smith (née Yeatman), Doreen and Derek Stanton, Leslie Thomas, Elsie Toms, Freda and the late Edgar Tory, John Tory, Linda Walbrin (née Damen), John Waterman, Nora Way and Susan Williams (née Churchill).

PREFACE

The Dorset village of Piddlehinton lies between chalk downs in the valley of the River Piddle, 5 miles north of Dorchester. It has a population of just over 400, a church, a post office and shop, a pub, a village hall (in the old village school) and a war memorial in the village centre where its two roads cross.

This book results from an exhibition of the history of the village we put on in the village hall at Easter 1988. We all became fascinated by the many bits of the historical jigsaw we were able to unearth. We spent many hours searching through records at the Dorset County Record Office, the County Library, the County Museum, Eton College Archives, Church House Westminster, and local lawyers' and estate agents' offices. Past and present residents of the village dug out relevant papers, photos and memories for us. We are much indebted to all these people who took a lot of time and trouble to help us.

Reluctant to let our exhibition become an archive itself, and fired by the tremendous enthusiasm for knowledge of Piddlehinton's past expressed by so many of the exhibition's visitors, we resolved to translate that exhibition into this book. It is but a small sample of some of the fascinating wealth of information we discovered that awaits more serious historians. It was our curiosity about life in Piddlehinton in previous centuries that led us on.

All history is the story of change and it continues to be told daily in Piddlehinton, as everywhere else. We hope you will enjoy this record of some aspects of change in Piddlehinton.

Susan Belgrave
Angela Drewe
Wendy Gregory
Naomi Smeeth
Tessa Spiller
Gillian Vickery
Judith Wardlaw

Photographic work by Julian Wardlaw

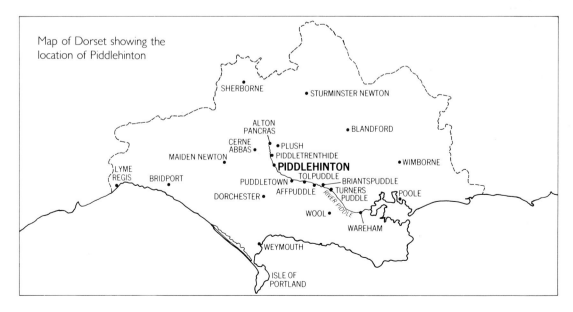

Map of Dorset showing the location of Piddlehinton

INTRODUCTION

By Robert Belgrave

It is a privilege for one born in Piddlehinton nearly 70 years ago to be asked to write an introduction to this short history of the village. The Village Hall Committee who initiated the project, and the smaller group who did the research and put together first an exhibition and then this book, are to be congratulated, not least for their timing. For there are still a few of us around who can remember the 1920s, which constitute a watershed in the history of the village.

If Robert, Count of Mortain (to whom his brother, William the Conqueror, gave the village in 1066), or the Provost of Eton in 1442 (the year in which Henry VI gave the village to his new school) had visited Piddlehinton in 1920, they would not have had much difficulty in understanding what was going on. Almost all work was still done by men and women in the village. You could get your horses shod, your shoes made, your house thatched, your hurdles, wagon wheels and your coffin made by Piddlehinton craftsmen.

There has been more change in village life since the 1914–18 war than in all the 830 years of recorded history before that date, when little that happened in the world outside affected the village. It did not matter much whether the absentee landlord was the king, a Norman abbey or an English school. There was never a squire here. Perhaps that is why there is a certain spirit of independence in the village, where people like to organize their own amusements.

A few outside events did have an impact. The Black Death in 1348 permanently wiped out whole hamlets in the parish. The prosperity of the Elizabethan era permitted the Churchill family to build a manor house at Muston. The development of water meadows in the eighteenth century made it possible to increase the number of sheep, and raise the tithes with which parson Montague rebuilt the Rectory. The enclosures of 1835 set the farm, field and woodland pattern we have today.

The agricultural depressions of the 1890s and 1930s drove people to look for jobs in the towns, or overseas, or in the armed forces. There has always been a tradition of service here. Indeed wars have probably been the biggest outside influence on the village.

It was the war of 1914–18, and the technological revolution that went with it, that dealt the most shattering blow to the pattern of village life. On the village War Memorial, there are seventeen names of men killed in that war, out of a total of fifty-six who served. Mercifully there were only four names to add after the 1939–45 war, partly because casualties were less, and partly because all those involved in food production were compelled to stay in order to save the nation from starvation. Many of them served also in the Home Guard which, however comic its activities seemed to the English, certainly impressed Hitler.

It would be a mistake, however, to think of the past as a sort of golden age. Life in the country was hard. Even in the 1930s some children were hungry, ill-clothed and ill-shod, and there was no electricity, piped water or sewer. It would be wrong to fossilize the history of Piddlehinton in a sort of romantic, Victorian dream out of a novel by Thomas Hardy. There has always been change; never more than in the last 70 years.

Chapter 1

EARLY HISTORY

Neolithic flint tools, late Bronze Age burial mounds, Iron Age and Roman field systems and a small late Roman or Dark Age cemetery; all these archaeological finds in our parish suggest that this land has been continuously inhabited since 4000 B.C. After the Roman withdrawal, the Saxons finally reached Wessex in the seventh century A.D. Our first documentary evidence comes from this period.

As the Saxon pagans converted to Christianity, so monasteries were founded with gifts of land for their upkeep. During the reign of King Athelstan (A.D. 925–939), one 'hide' of land at Little Puddle was granted to the Abbot of Milton. From A.D. 959 to 975, King Edgar established and restored many monasteries. Lands at Muston were granted to Cerne Abbey upon its founding. In 966, Edgar confirmed a gift of land at 'Uppidelen', to the church and nuns of Shaftesbury. Although this may refer to a tithing in Piddletrenthide, later documents record that it was seized by King Harold and then passed into the hands of the Count of Mortain after the Norman invasion.

With the Norman invasion in 1066 the picture changed, and for the next 351 years the Manor of Piddlehinton was the property of Robert, Count of Mortain and of the collegiate church he founded. His half-brother William had created him Count of Mortain in 1055. He always consulted Robert about all his plans including the projected invasion of England.

After the Norman victory at the Battle of Hastings, William became King of England. He claimed all the land as his own and gave much of it to his Norman friends and relations. Robert was given the biggest share – 973 manors – making him the richest landowner in England, apart from the Church. Seventy of his manors were in Dorset including Blandford, Spetisbury, Child Okeford, Hanford, Bryanston and Piddlehinton.

In 1082, Robert and his wife Mathilde founded the collegiate church of St Evroult, inside their castle at Mortain. They endowed it with many of Robert's properties in England, including Piddlehinton.

△
Map to show the location of Mortain in Normandy in relation to Piddlehinton, and the route of the Norman invasion in 1066

◁
This section of the Bayeux Tapestry shows William the Conqueror conferring with his two half-brothers, Robert, Count of Mortain, and Odo, Bishop of Bayeux, before the Battle of Hastings

By 1086 Piddlehinton was a thriving, if small, manor as recorded in the Domesday Book.

> The Abbot of Marmoutier holds Piddlehinton from the Count [of Mortain]. Two thanes held it before 1066 as two manors.
> It paid tax for 10 hides. Land for 7 ploughs of which 5 hides are in lordship; 2 ploughs there; 3 slaves; 13 villagers and 8 smallholders with 3 ploughs.
> Meadow 33 acres; pasture 15 furlongs
> Value £10

Unfortunately all the records of Mortain, which since the French Revolution had been kept at the provincial capital of St Lo, were destroyed in June 1944 during the allied invasion of Normandy. We do know, however, that the collegiate church of Mortain, by then an abbey, still owned Piddlehinton in 1417. It was in that year, after the Battle of Agincourt, that Henry V decided to confiscate the English estates of the 'alien priories' of France. It was thus that Piddlehinton became the property of the King of England after 351 years as a French possession. The king entrusted it to the Augustinian Priory at Christchurch. The Manorial Court which administered it was held in Puddletown, which was already connected with Christchurch Priory.

Chapter 2

ETON COLLEGE AS LORDS OF THE MANOR

In 1440, when he was eighteen, Henry VI founded 'the King's College of the Blessed Virgin Mary', at Eton. He endowed it with sixty-seven of his properties including, 'A farm and rent of £14. 8. 4. of Hynepidell otherwise called Pydelhyngton with its appurtenances'.

By the time that the Provost and Fellows of Eton College became Lords of the Manor of Piddlehinton, the relationship between the lord and the people living on manorial land had evolved to the stage where rents had replaced services as the basis for granting land. The land in the Manor of Piddlehinton was of two categories:

1. The Lord's desmesne, or Manor Farm as we know it, comprising by far the largest acreage, let on a lease, usually of 21 years. The tenant needed to be a man of some means and the tenancy carried certain duties.
2. The holdings granted for fixed rents with hereditary rights to the villagers. These were entered in the manorial records. A copy of the entry was given to the tenant, whose holding was then referred to as a copyhold.

Copyhold tenants based the length of their leases on the longest of three lives nominated by them. In 1750, William Rogers, aged 28, a Piddlehinton blacksmith, took a lease in conjunction with his brother Robert, aged 30, a shoemaker of Bridport, and Robert's son Samuel, aged 5, 'for the term of their lives and the longest liver of them successively'. Copyhold tenancies gradually gave way to annual tenancies. The last copyhold tenancy in Piddlehinton was given in 1893.

An 'heriot' was paid to Eton College when a tenant surrendered his tenancy, or died, and a 'fine' or lump sum was due when the college gave a new lease.

Eton College appointed the rector. They were also responsible for ensuring the smooth running of the village through their Manorial Court, carrying out many of the roles of Justices of the Peace and local councillors today. They had some financial responsibilities as well. The account from the steward, Francis Ingram, to the college in 1838 included, 'Allowed Thomas Sansom towards the repair of Well 1s. 0d. Mr Martin's Bill for Map of Piddlehinton £34. 10s. 0d.'

Lordship of the Manor of Piddlehinton did not include ownership of all the land in the village however. There were a few freeholders who were not obliged to attend the Manorial Court and who were subject to the common law of the Royal Courts. They paid only a token rent to Eton College. Among the recorded freemen in Piddlehinton were:

Seventeenth century – George Romayne and Joseph Beck.
Eighteenth century – Christopher White and William Beck.
Nineteenth century – Stephen Iles, Thomas Harris, Robert Devenish, The Rev. W. H. Churchill, John Baverstock Knight and Gen. Charles Astell.

To convene the court, Eton sent a steward and a clerk to Piddlehinton and gave notice that a court would be held. In later years they appointed a local steward, often a lawyer from Dorchester, to act for them. Records show that courts took place once in most years. Every male over the age of twelve had a duty to be present. Anyone who failed to do so was fined.

The Manorial Court was divided into two parts. The Court Leet dealt with petty offences, highway and ditch disrepair, and enforcement of the law relating to the sale of ale, etc. The Court Baron enforced the customs of the Manor on the lord's property. These customs varied from manor to manor and were seldom committed to paper; they rested on oral tradition. They covered the surrender and renewal of tenancies, the use of the common fields and many other aspects of village life. Through these courts the Lord of the Manor controlled the economic life of the villagers down to the most homely details.

Each year when the court met, a jury of twelve people was elected. It had a duty to appoint two constables, a tithing man, a hayward and two people holding the offices of the viewers of hedges and the tellers of cattle.

It was for the jury to present to the steward those who had committed petty crimes. Fines were imposed, swelling the lord's coffers. A great many of the items presented to the court were connected with ensuring that the unwritten farming customs of the community were followed. Here are three examples:

1683 'Wee present that our high wayes and bridges are well repaired, except the bridge in the Court Close which belongs to Nicholas Kelway to bee repaired. Ordered that the said Nicholas Kelway putt a sufficient planck over the river for passage by Allhallowtide upon paine of 12 pence.'

1727 'We present John Cole for annoying our watercourse by placing a hogstye across the same and not removing this stye though formerly by us presented and ordered that he remove the stye therefrom in a month on payment of 22s.'

1869 'We present Charles Grey a Copyhold tenant of this Liberty and manor and also Hayward of the same who owes suit and service at this Court and hath made default in attending same and we amend him in the sum of 6d.'

The other important function of the Manorial Court was to record the surrender and admittance to tenancies. The Manor Farm was usually let on a 21-year lease, and the same family often renewed the tenancy as this list shows.

1529–1568 John, Owen, Elizabeth and Henry Hyllary
1568–1622 Henry and Edward Lowman
1630–1786 Nicholas, Christopher, John, James and Elizabeth Kellaway
1786–1821 Thomas Meggs
1822–1880 William, George, Charles and George Mayo
1880–1885 Joseph Roper
1885–1922 Levi and Joseph Riggs
1922–1939 Henry Smart
1939–1945 Thomas Fellowes
1945–1966 Rex Lovelace (also tenant of East Farm)

Some of them installed sub-tenants to run their farm for them, but they all were closely involved with the affairs of Piddlehinton.

The tenancy of the desmesne lands also carried certain obligations. These included the provision of lodgings for visiting Eton officials and their horses, and the collecting of rents from the copyhold tenants of the cottages. In 1738 Nicholas Kellaway complained that the rents he collected added up to only £12. 3s. 4d. a year, whereas the college expected £13. 12s. 10d. 'If you please to examine Mr Crow's Survey', he wrote to the Provost of Eton, 'you will find ev'ry one's Lord's rent upon their respective Copies exactly agree with the Rent Role wch. I send you inclos'd. I assure you we do not collect one Farthing more nay often loose sevral Shillings of that through the poverty of the Cottagery.'

The Cottagery in Piddlehinton had long been poor and remained so for a further 200 years. The more prosperous yeomen farmers gradually took over the uneconomic smallholdings, employing the previous tenants as labourers. In 1620, out of a population of 216, there were thirty-two farms. By 1841 the census records only six farms, although the population was 394. Ninety-five people were listed as agricultural labourers or in other jobs directly connected with farming. The rest of the population were engaged in crafts or in servicing the village. This transition was in large measure due to the enclosing of the shared open farmland.

In 1620, part of the desmesne farm was enclosed, in spite of the strong protests of the thirty-one tenant farmers, including the rector, who farmed 40 acres of Glebe. The desmesne farm at that date comprised 136 acres; twenty copyhold tenants had 24 acres each, and another ten tenants had 12 acres each. They all shared common grazing on the unenclosed downs; some also had rights in a water meadow on the River Frome.

Later, the 1835 Piddlehinton Enclosure Act imposed a complete change on the villagers' way of life. Their rights to graze animals, grow crops and gather furze for fuel in the three main village fields and other common land were removed as these were enclosed. It saw the advent of the tied cottage and introduced the landscape pattern of hedges and fences with which we have become familiar.

Gradually the Lord of the Manor ceased to have such social and economic importance in the lives of the villagers, as the administration of justice and local government passed to other bodies. The few remaining duties and privileges were ended by Act of Parliament in 1922.

In 1966, Eton College sold its land in Piddlehinton, and many of its houses, to Mr Ingram Spencer of Hanford Farms. Eton College had owned the Manor of Piddlehinton for 524 years. We do not know how different were the boundaries of the manor they sold from those of the manor given to them by Henry VI, but the village itself had changed a great deal. After 1966, Eton College retained only the right to appoint the rector, which it still has.

Chapter 3

PROPERTIES NOT OWNED BY ETON COLLEGE

To the south of the Manor of Piddlehinton, within the parish, lies a block of land which was not owned by Eton, and has a separate history to that of the manorial estates.

One part was the Manor of Little Puddle or Piddle. In 1086, as recorded in the Domesday Book, it was part of the Royal Manor of Puddletown, and continued in this parish until 1885. Most of this manor belonged to King William, but seems always to have been let, and later owned, in two parts. One part was held for some years by Christchurch Priory, who also held other lands in Puddletown. The other manors in the parish, as we know it today, were owned in 1086 by the Count of Mortain, and included Combe Deverel and North Lovard or Loffard. Cerne Abbey owned Muston Manor until the Dissolution. Although at the time of the Domesday Book these manors were thriving settlements, today they are represented as farms with perhaps a single farmhouse, and rough outlines of house foundations in the middle of a field. The blame for small settlement desertion is often laid on the plague, which reached Britain in 1348, via Weymouth. Evidence suggests, however, that the population was already declining by this time.

Little Puddle

In the thirteenth century this manor had a population sufficient to work their own manorial system, with a custom of services attached to their holdings. There is even a thirteenth-century reference to an independent chapel here, which was claimed in the fourteenth century by the vicar of Puddletown. Thereafter, Christchurch Priory allowed for the upkeep of Puddletown church a portion of the tithes of hay in Little Puddle and pasture for '100 sheep, 5 cows and 10 hogs'. After the Dissolution, when the lands were held privately, the vicar of Puddletown still retained the right to pasture 100 sheep in the manor.

References to later private holdings are confusing, but perhaps

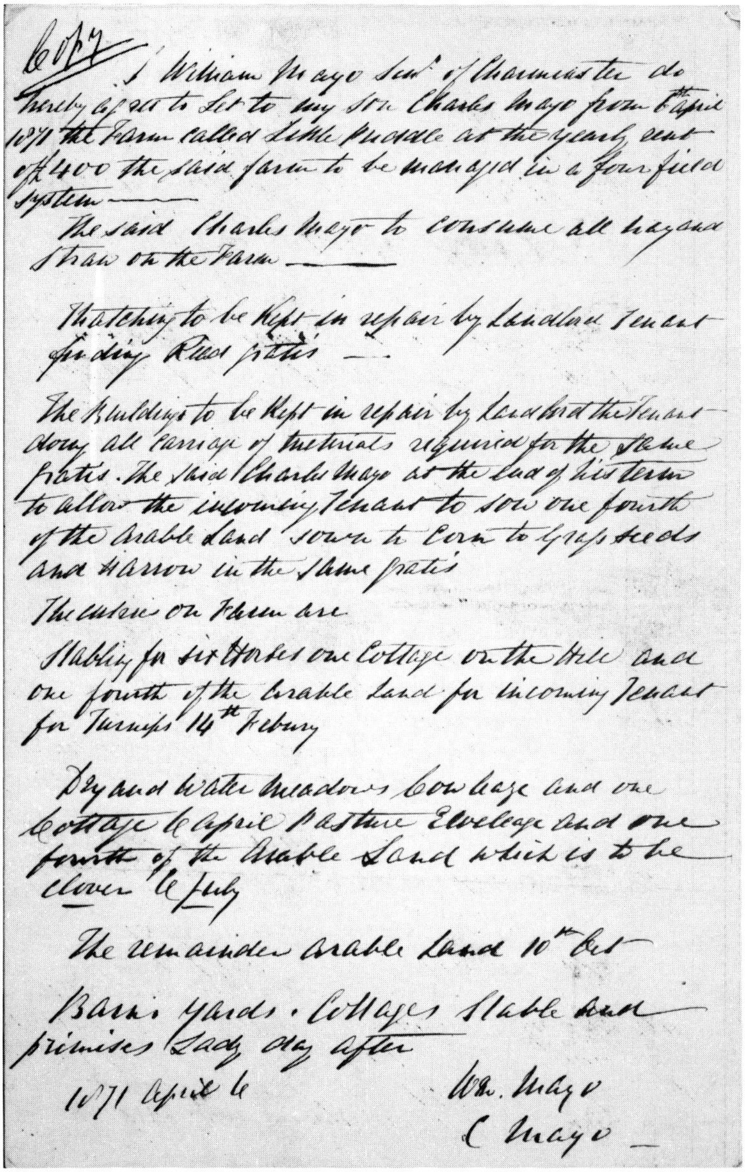

[Handwritten agreement document — transcription of legible portions:]

Copy

I William Mayo Sen.ʳ of Charminster do hereby agree to Let to my Son Charles Mayo from April 1871 the Farm called Little Puddle at the yearly rent of £400 the said farm to be managed in a Four field system

The said Charles Mayo to consume all hay and straw on the Farm —

Thatching to be kept in repair by Landlord Tenant finding Rods spetis —

The Buildings to be kept in repair by Landlord the Tenant doing all Carriage of materials required for the same gratis. The said Charles Mayo at the end of his term to allow the incoming Tenant to sow one fourth of the arable land sown to Corn to Grass seeds and Harrow in the same gratis

The entries on Farm are

Stabling for six Horses one Cottage on the Hill and one fourth of the Arable Land for incoming Tenant for Turnips 14ᵗʰ Febuary

Dry and Water Meadows, Cow leaze and one Cottage 6 April Pasture Ewe leaze and one fourth of the Arable Land which is to be clover 6 July

The remainder arable Land 10ᵗʰ Oct

Barns yards . Cottages Stable and premises Lady day after

1871 April 6   Wm. Mayo
                                C Mayo —

◁

Agreement of the Mayo family. In the mid-nineteenth century William's son (another William) let Little Puddle to his brother Charles. The latter retired and William's third son, Charles, took the tenancy. This agreement is dated 6 April 1871. Annual rent at this time was £400. The younger Charles died, aged only 44, in 1893

The elder Charles Mayo is on the left and is with Rev. Roper. Charles' brother William bought his land after Charles' death. William himself died in 1875. His son William took up the option to buy these farms for £5000. Thereafter the younger Charles' rent for Little Puddle, Holcombe and Blackhouse was £700

▽

from the Dissolution, the northern half of Bourne Farm was held with Muston lands. The southern half, Little Puddle Farm, seems to have had a connection with the Piddlehinton desmesne farmers. It is certain that Thomas Meggs owned it. By his death in 1819 there were only two houses left near the medieval site. Ownership then passed to the Mayo family – who also rented the desmesne farm. William Mayo came from Steepleton and lived at Little Puddle for a while. As the family acquired land in other parts of Dorset, younger

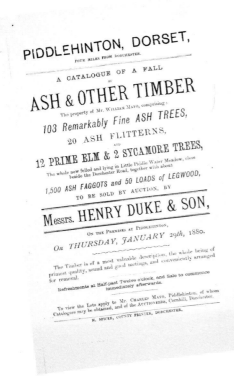

In 1880 the Mayo family held a large sale of timber. This may have included wood brought from other Mayo farms. The 132 lots made £107. In 1886 Charles Mayo quitted the farm. His sale included over 1000 Dorset Down sheep and lambs, six cart horses and a hack horse

brothers and sons rented Little Puddle Farm. In 1874 the family acquired Holcombe and Blackhouse Farms in Piddlehinton, when Charles Mayo died.

The Mayos continued to farm here until 1941. During the nineteenth century they primarily ran a sheep farm. A dairy herd was established in the 1920s. A small acreage of arable – rye, barley, wheat, oats, vetch and mangolds – was grown for fodder. There was an orchard, and cider was made until the 1930s. When Mr Paul bought the farm it became almost entirely arable, although today the Holland family have a dairy herd once more.

During the nineteenth century the population of Little Puddle increased once again, as the Mayos built farm cottages for their workmen. In the 1930s they bought Dales Corner with a house, which had been sold separately from the Muston estate. This was used as the main farmhouse. Little Puddle farmhouse has since been sold, and the nineteenth-century cottages are decayed.

Len Maidment, who lived at Little Puddle farmhouse, milked by hand the Red Devon herd at a new dairy built at Dales Corner. In 1921, only fifteen heifers were recorded on the farm. Twenty years later, there were twenty-five dairy cows, twenty-three heifers, five calves and five bulls   ▽

△
From 1913 until 1941, Henry George Mayo, pictured here outside Little Puddle farmhouse, farmed the land – although he lived at Corton Farm, Portesham. Ben Cheeseman remembers him riding from there to Little Puddle on horseback, always wearing his bowler hat

◁
The Cheesemans lived and worked at Little Puddle for many years. Before that they worked at Muston. Here is Fred Cheeseman, the carter, with three of the four horses from his Little Puddle Hill stable, ploughing at Holcombe in 1941. There was another stable of three horses at Holcombe

◁
Fred Cheeseman is pictured here with the threshing contractor Percy Pile, who came to the farm in the 1930s from Godmanstone. Fred lived in a cottage on Little Puddle Hill which has since been pulled down. Harry Cheeseman, the farm foreman, lived next door

Nappers Mite Farm, Bourne Farm and Muston Manor

Nappers Mite Farm, included in the Puddletown parish until the reform of the parish boundaries, has an unusual history, although we can only trace it from the seventeenth century when it was bought by Sir Robert Napper. Sir Robert and his son built an almshouse in Dorchester and Robert's will stated that the farm at Little Puddle was to be leased at a yearly rent of £50, and that money was to be used for the 'sustenation and maintenance of the almshouse and ten poor men'. This almshouse, with its distinctive building, can still be seen in South Street in Dorchester, and is still known as 'Nappers Mite', despite being redeveloped as shops. Nappers Mite Farm itself has been known by various names, derived from its charity connections – Alms Farm, Aims Barn, and latterly, Puddletown Farm.

In 1892, Mr Harold Waterman, who already held the tenancy of Bourne Farm, also took over the 168 acres of Nappers Mite Farm. For a year and a half he ran both farms with mixed fortune. He put a great deal of effort into them, hoping that he would continue to farm them both for several years. He lodged at the Piddlehinton Manor farmhouse whilst waiting for a new house to be built at Bourne (the farmhouse there had been divided into farmworkers' dwellings). In 1894, he wanted to marry Elizabeth Wright of Dorchester, but as the house at Bourne did not materialize, he took the tenancy of a farm at Alton Pancras where a house was available. He left Bourne Farm in 1894, but kept on Nappers Mite Farm until the end of 1896. He died in 1923 and both he and his wife are buried at Piddlehinton.

Bourne Farm had been bought by the Churchill family, perhaps with the Muston estate in the seventeenth century. In 1824, a valuation of Puddletown lands details Bourne as a mixed farm of 164 acres tenanted by Mr George Burt, who was still there in 1839. During Mr Waterman's time at Bourne, he built up the road from Bourne Drove across the 'New Piece' field to the Bourne buildings. He also had the pond at Bourne rebuilt.

Mr Waterman employed a lot of local casual labour and as a member of the Puddletown division of the Technical Instruction Committee, he kept an interest in his employees and entered them in local competitions. Joseph White was entered in a 'Hoeing and Hedging' competition, and Samuel Stack in a 'Shepherding' competition.

As well as having a dairy, Mr Waterman sold pigs locally, and Dorset Horn sheep, poultry and eggs at Dorchester Market. Rabbits were an important additional 'crop'. He also had barley to sell to Hall & Woodhouse Brewery at Ansty, and some straw for thatching.

The original Muston Manor was that which had been granted to Cerne Abbey until the Dissolution, when John Bartlett, alias Hancock, purchased it with other abbey lands. In his hands it

△
Harold Waterman was advised to take up farming for his health. He came from Kent to work as a farm pupil at Manor Farm, Piddlehinton. He obtained the lease of Bourne Farm in 1890, and Nappers Mite Farm in 1892

continued to be leased by the Lowman family, the desmesne farmers of Piddlehinton. The Bartlett family sold it in 1609 to John Churchill, whose father had already bought the small manor of North Lovard, to the south-west.

Clement Tory bought Muston Manor and its 980 acres of farmland from the Trustees of William Churchill's estate in 1906. Although he did not live in the farmhouse, he took an active part in the farming of the land.

When Clement Tory died on 4 February 1940, he left 2700 acres of land stretching from Dorchester to Melcombe Horsey. All the land was sold off and two of Clement's sons bought part of the estate at Piddlehinton. Edgar bought Bourne Farm, which he farmed for 23 years.

◁▽
Clement Tory owned the steam threshing and binding machines which are photographed here in about 1918. The Overtine tractor (below) was later buried on land now part of Lea Farm. Rex Lovelace dug it up to retrieve the large water tanks, but the rest remains buried to this day

△
Doles Wood Plantation was bought by Clement Tory, who sold it in 1940 for £325. Edgar Tory bought it back in 1945 for £1 more. The shooting party here includes Philip Tory, Elneth Lovelace, Edgar Tory, Nancy Lovelace, Blanche Tory, Brian Needham and Clement Tory

▷
The first combine harvester was bought during the Second World War by Rex Lovelace and Edgar Tory, who between them had the 400 acres of corn required to qualify for a combine. The Massey Harris, costing £1138, arrived from Canada in boxes and was assembled by Reg Cosh

▷
Bags of corn are collected after combining. The combine needed two operators. The bagger, behind the driver, placed and removed bags from four outlets – two main corn, one tailings and one dust bag. Edgar later bought out Rex's share. The combine finished its days in the trees at Doles Wood

The Churchills have the longest known connection with Piddlehinton of any family. They originally came over from Normandy with William the Conqueror. From these first members of the family were descended not only the John Churchill who bought Muston Manor in 1609, but also the John Churchill who became the first Duke of Marlborough, and, through him, Winston Churchill. Over the centuries many Churchills were baptized, married, and buried in Piddlehinton church. Several Churchills of Muston were High Sheriffs of the County of Dorset. They owned Muston Manor for 297 years until 1906, although Cdr K. and Mrs Churchill bought the house back in 1915.

Susan, Cdr and Mrs Churchill's daughter, married Mark Williams of Bridehead in 1941. Because of the war, their wedding was not in Piddlehinton (as had been those of so many Churchills in previous generations), but in Dorchester. It was held on a Saturday morning so that their many friends could combine coming to the wedding with a Dorchester shopping trip, making double use of their scarce wartime petrol coupons.

The Churchills' son, John, sold the house to Mr and Mrs O. B. N. Paine in 1976, after Cdr Churchill's death.

Prior to the Second World War, the young Margaret Jeanes of Piddlehinton was employed at Muston Manor, first as housemaid and then as parlour maid. Also employed were a cook and a housemaid, as well as the gardener, who lived in the Gardener's Cottage. Margaret worked from 7 a.m. until 9.30 p.m., with half a

△
The Rev. W. R. H. Churchill and his wife Martha. Rev. Churchill (1774–1847), rector of Winterbourne Stickland, who inherited this large estate, also invested in a lot of other property in the village, both farmland and houses. He did not live at Muston Manor, but took great interest in his estates

Almost certainly the Churchills built Muston Manor in the seventeenth century, but within 80 years they had moved into Dorchester, having bought Colliton, now the site of County Hall. The original building would probably have looked like this watercolour painting from around 1800. The house has since been extended

day a week and every other Sunday off. On her half day off, she walked to Piddlehinton for tea with her mother, and then walked back to Muston again, that was the afternoon gone!

During the war Cdr Churchill was called on to the Reserve List. Mrs Churchill stayed at Muston and did VAD work. Evacuees were billeted at the house, and also the padre from the camp rented part of the house. The house staff was reduced to just Margaret until she too was called up.

▷ Cdr Kenneth Churchill (a descendant of the last William Churchill to own Muston) and his wife lived at Muston from 1915. They lived there for the rest of their lives and became prominent and respected inhabitants of the village. Cdr Churchill was for many years a churchwarden and a school manager

▷ Margaret Churchill was an enthusiastic supporter of the Women's Institute. Among many other activities, she organized a home knitting industry in the village

△
Margaret Jeanes looked after the land girls in their hostel at Piddletrenthide for six months, until she found a placement. Two girls, Joan Davis and Irene Cordier, worked at Muston and are pictured here

LAND GIRL KILLED WHEN TRACTOR SKIDS
Dorset Coroner's Advice To Farmers At Inquest

THE need for care in the use of tractors was mentioned by the acting Coroner for South Dorset (Mr. P. M. Wickham) at an inquest at Dorchester, yesterday arising out of an accident at Puddlehinton which caused the death of a land girl.

"I don't wish to make this a particular instance," he said, "but it is incumbent upon all farmers to take great care to see just what their tractors can do. Unfortunately, this is not the first accident of this nature which has occurred in this district lately and I do feel that, perhaps, we are rather inclined to use our tractors for things they are not capable of doing. I know speed is a big question in these days, but obviously we have to make sure that everything is safe."

PINNED BENEATH TRAILER

The inquest was upon 20-years-old Miss Joan Edith Davis, a London girl who was killed when a trailer drawn by a tractor overturned during harvesting at Muston Farm, Puddlehinton, pinning her beneath the trailer. A verdict of Death by Misadventure was recorded.

It was stated by Dr. W. G. Bendle, resident medical officer at the County Hospital, Dorchester, that the girl was dead when admitted to hospital shortly after noon on Tuesday, death being due to suffocation owing to severe compression of the lower part of the chest.

The young woman's father, George Davis, of 19, Ivor-street, Royal College-street, Camden Town, London, said she was a cinema cashier before joining the Land Army a year and a half ago. "She had been at Puddletrenthide all the time and liked it very much," he added.

TRACTOR SKIDDED ON WET GRASS

Wilfred Vincent, son of Mr. Gaius Vincent, of Muston Farm, stated that on Tuesday he was working on a field known as Lower Ground, carrying wheat. He was driving the tractor at the time of the accident. It had been driven by Joan Davis earlier in the day. Behind the tractor were a trailer and a waggon, both carrying sheaves, and the load had to be taken into the next field, where there was a stack.

The field was fairly level, but on leaving it there was a slope. Before reaching the gate it was the practice to stop and chain up the wheels of the waggon, but when he applied the brakes to stop the tractor it failed to stop by reason of the smoothness of the grass. The brakes were working properly, but the wheels skidded when they locked. The tractor went on and gradually gathered speed, and the only thing he could do was to try to keep it straight. Suddenly it turned round and he was thrown off.

ANOTHER GIRL JUMPED OFF

He picked himself up—he had a bruised shoulder—and found that the tractor had come to a standstill and the trailer had turned over. Miss Davis, who had been on the tractor with him, was underneath the trailer. The tractor had rubber tyres. When tested afterwards the brakes proved to be in good order.

Bertie E. House, of Muston Farm, who was walking behind the waggon, said he saw the wheels of the tractor start to slide and afterwards saw the trailer tip over.

Miss Irene Cordier, a land girl, who was riding on the shafts of the waggon behind the trailer, said she wondered why they did not stop at the gate and noticed that they were gathering speed. She jumped off and fell underneath the waggon, and one of her hands was hurt.

Efforts were made to move the trailer from Miss Davis, who was unconscious and breathing rather heavily, but after about three or four minutes her breathing ceased. P.C. Webb spoke to finding the tractor facing up the hill about 5 yards from the gate, and stated there was a skid mark on the grass for this distance.

DIED IN SERVING NATION

After recording his verdict and expressing sympathy with the girl's father, the Coroner said, "She chose a form of National Service which is by no means the least arduous and has died in the course of it."

Mr. H. O. Lock, who attended on behalf of Mr. Vincent, associated himself with the Coroner's sympathy, and Miss Bonar, county secretary for the Women's Land Army, added, "We have lost a very good worker and the girls a very popular colleague."

▷
Tragically Joan Davis was killed in a farm accident as reported on 13 August 1943, in the *Dorset County Chronicle*

Robert Vincent of Waterston Manor Farm bought Muston Farm from Clement Tory during the First World War. Robert's son, Gaius, farmed there. In 1918, Robert bought Waterston Mead at a price of £45 per acre. The land was previously known as Lovard Mead, and later as Horse Ground. He built Snowdrop House here for his retirement. Later the Vincents bought the higher 60 acres, and made a farm for Howard Charles Vincent. He moved into Lea Farm in 1937.

△

Charlie Vincent with his farmworker Roy Percy and Margaret Jeanes, who worked at Lea Farm from January 1943. Two horses were kept to pull the two spring wagons and a large hay wagon. Margaret worked from 6.00 a.m. until 5.30 p.m., and was paid 1s. per hour. The farm was mainly dairy

△

Margaret Jeanes, here in her uniform in 1943, met her future husband whilst he was stationed at the camp. His regiment swapped camps with the Americans at Evershot and then he departed to prepare for D-Day. The couple married in Piddlehinton in 1945

Gardener's Cottage

The Gale family were carpenters, and for a while lived in the cottage at Muston. When they moved there, Mr Burch, the tenant farmer, had a saw pit dug. Mr Gale built wagons, doing everything himself, from felling trees to making the iron rims on the wheels. He even painted his name on the side in beautiful script. Like any other boys, John Gale's sons were often up to mischief and once, two of them painted Mr Burch's pig red, white and blue to honour Edward VII's coronation. The family later moved to Piddlehinton.

△
The Gale family at Muston. The photograph shows Fanny Gale and her daughter (Ethel?), John (in the large hat), and one of the workmen (in the apron). The reason for the large 'saw hat' is that when sawing a large trunk, one man stood on top with a cross cut saw, and the other man, in the pit, would keep the saw steady. The dust obviously fell on the man underneath so the large hat, often with a net or old curtain draped over it, kept the dust off him

Chapter 4

THE PARISH CHURCH OF ST MARY THE VIRGIN

The parish church lies at the heart of the village. The Civil Parish of Piddlehinton contains five original settlements: Piddlehinton, Coombe Deverel, Little Piddle, Muston and North Lovard. Until 1885, Little Piddle was part of Puddletown parish ▽

The first rector listed was William Gascely in 1295, under the patronage of the prior of Mortain. A church was dedicated to St Mary the Virgin in 1299, but only the west arch of the south tower of that original building still remains. There are also fourteenth-century remains of a cross and a coffin lid with a moulded edge, situated on the west wall. The south tower and south aisle date from the latter half of the fifteenth century. During the early sixteenth century, the chancel, north colonnade of the nave and south porch were added.

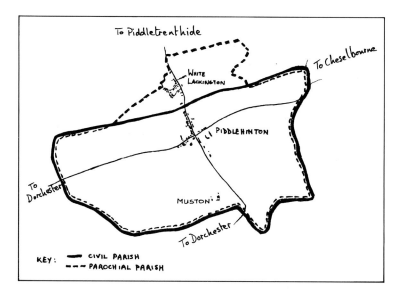

◁
The Parochial Parish of Piddlehinton includes the hamlet of White Lackington, which lies north of the village in the Civil Parish of Piddletrenthide. It can only be assumed that it was quicker to walk the 1 mile to St Mary's at Piddlehinton, than the 2 miles to All Saints' at Piddletrenthide

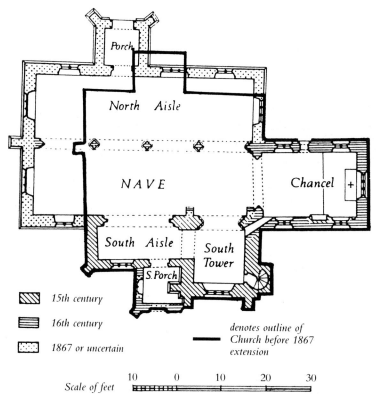

15th century

16th century

1867 or uncertain

denotes outline of Church before 1867 extension

Scale of feet   10   0   10   20   30

△
An unusual feature in the south wall of the chancel is the sedilia. This dates from the late fifteenth century and is a recess consisting of three stone seats to accommodate the priest, deacon and sub-deacon. The back of the sedilia has three stone panels with side standards and an overhanging cornice

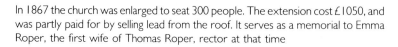

In 1867 the church was enlarged to seat 300 people. The extension cost £1050, and was partly paid for by selling lead from the roof. It serves as a memorial to Emma Roper, the first wife of Thomas Roper, rector at that time

◁

One of the oldest memorials in the church commemorates 'Master Wyllyam Goldynge 1562', listed as William Goldwyn, rector from 1550 to 1562. This rare brass is a 'palimpsest' – a brass having an inscription on both sides. A replica of the reverse is mounted beside it and shows the likeness of an abbot

▷

The tower, shown in this painting by Mary Hardy, the village schoolmistress and sister of Thomas Hardy, contains a peal of six bells. The tenor (1633) and second (1683) are the oldest. The third bell is dated 1721. The newest bell, the treble, was added as a memorial to Cdr Charles Swayne RN, in 1950

◁

The old oil lamps shown in this photograph were replaced by electric lighting in 1938. This pulpit was replaced after 1927

◁
The turret clock, bought in 1730, was made by Lawrence Boyce of Puddletown and can still be seen in the church today. It would have had a pendulum for two weights, and it had to be wound every day, a responsibility of the clerk for which he was paid 12s. a year. The clock's time-keeping was checked by the sun-dial on the south wall of the church. The clock was still in use in the church in 1760

In recent years, local families have contributed much to the furnishings of the church. In 1925 the font area was railed off and carpeted by Cdr and Mrs Churchill to commemorate the baptism of their daughter Susan. It had been over 200 years since a member of the Churchill family had been christened in Piddlehinton. In 1927 the Churchills donated the communion table, panelling and stalls in the chancel in memory of their seven-year-old son, George. The nave choir stalls commemorate Gwladys and John Belgrave of West Lodge, who worshipped here from 1917 to 1955. The pulpit was given in memory of Walter Lovelace in 1927, and the church gates in 1950, in memory of Mrs Walter Lovelace.

Some Rectors of Piddlehinton

Thomas Browne – Rector 1590–1617

Thomas Clavering – Rector 1629–1665

Thomas Clavering's wife, Martha, died from the plague while ministering to the sick of the parish in 1664. On the north wall of the chancel, painted in wood and inscribed in Latin, is a sentimental memorial to her. The translation is underneath the memorial and worth quoting:

> John, first-born son of Thomas Clavering, sweet infant babe, taken away from his mother's bosom, was laid low on the 18th day of April, 1644, and with him is laid Martha, the most devoted mother of the said child and of nine children more. A wife most faithful to her husband, she was descended from the families of the Souths of Swallowcliff, in the county of Wilts, and of the Butlers of the county of Dorset. She was a cheerful housewife, a matron of

△
The brass engraving in the chancel depicts Thomas Browne, who defended the poor against the landlords when they wanted the desmesne farmer to enclose part of the common meadow. It was unusual for a rector to consider the needs of the poor above those of the landlords and tenants. The inscription on the brass reads:

Here lieth interred the body of Mr Thomas Browne, Clerke who lived parson of this place seaven and twentie yeares and beinge sixtie and seaven yeares old departed this lyfe the fourth day of October 1617

spotless chastity, most prudent, calm and gracious. In beauty of bodily form and of mind she was lovely and lovable. In pressing forward every good work she was at once most ready herself in its pursuit, and likewise instigated others to follow it. In her piety she was neither ostentatious nor superficial, but in a natural manner religious and inwardly devoted to her God. A lady of most engaging manners, combined with serious behaviour, she attached to herself all who knew her by loving and dutiful service. Whatsoever accident might befall, she manifested a quiet and unruffled spirit resigned to the will of her Heavenly Father. Worthy she was above all others to be held in perpetual remembrance and her example deserves to be followed as a pattern. The dearest, congenial and most deeply lamented spouse. While with a too ready and forward kindliness she was intent on caring diligently for the health of others, thinking alas too little of her own, she was seized by the malignant epidemic disease which she was busily engaged in tending. She cast herself resolutely upon the arms of the Saviour Jesus, and on a night which was so sad a time for us, but for herself the Dawning of the Day, on May 22nd 1664, she fell asleep gently in the Lord in the course of her six and fortieth year. It was her husband's wish to ascribe to her memory this record of their unbroken harmony, and of her worth which cannot ever be sufficiently extolled, as a tribute which Truth and Love demand. In his bereavement he is forlorn, rendered inevitably a sorrowing mourner: like the night raven wakeful in the house, or as the sparrow left alone upon the housetop.

T.C. her husband. She has gone before. I shall follow. We shall live again. Nay! He who wrote the preceding lines has now already followed to the place whither he taught her to lead the way. Mr Thomas Clavering, the excellent Rector and Ornament of this Church, dying on the 29th October, in the year of our Lord 1665, in the 66th year of his age.

Thow knowest not at what hour: therefore watch.

Canon Thomas Thellusson Carter – Rector 1838–1844

Canon Carter made himself unpopular by stopping the Piddlehinton Dole. The Dole had been a tradition for many years and had cost the rectors £9 or £10 per annum, from their own pockets.

The Dole consisted of 1 lb. of bread, a mince pie (large enough to be cut into four), and 1 pt. of ale, to be handed out to every parishioner at Christmastide (6 January).

In 1839, Canon Carter considered this was too costly and wasteful, so he told his congregation that he would discontinue the Dole and substitute a Relief Fund, including the gift of blankets, to the poor. This was an unpopular decision, particularly with the wealthier parishioners, who considered the Dole their right. Canon Carter was forced to appeal to the Provost and Fellows of Eton College. He won his case and brought in his Relief Fund.

△
Canon Carter. The east window of the chancel was installed in 1845 in memory of Canon Carter. It depicts the Good Shepherd, St Peter and St Mary the Virgin

His opponents were angry and withheld their tithes, smashed some windows in the chancel, which were Canon Carter's responsibility, and generally made his life most unpleasant. Eventually Canon Carter was forced to leave the village in 1844. The Dole was distributed once again in 1989, 150 years later, but not at the rector's expense!

William George Newman – Rector 1908–1938

John Chaloner Chute – Rector 1938–1957

△
Rev. and Mrs Newman. William Newman was rector of Piddlehinton during the First World War. He was a West Country man who enjoyed rural life. He was known to be an excellent shot and never missed a rabbit

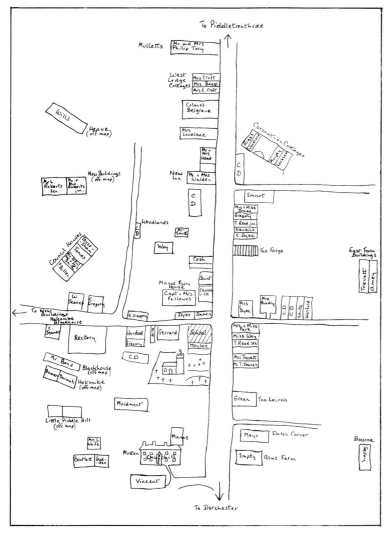

△
On arrival at Piddlehinton, in order to aid his memory, Jack Chute drew this plan of the village

△
John Chute graduated from Balliol College, Oxford, was ordained priest and eventually became a housemaster at Eton. On retiring from Eton, he was given the living at Piddlehinton. Jack and Mamie Chute were a gentle and popular couple who led active roles in village life

Overseers of the Poor

△

The overseers dealt with the 'First Poor' of the village, and casual charity to those passing through was paid by the churchwardens. There was a highly mobile population especially during the seventeenth and eighteenth centuries. The churchwardens' accounts of this period show payments ranging from 2d. to 2s. to seamen, fire victims, soldiers, cripples and licensed travellers. Seamen were often Dutch, or redeemed from 'Turkish Slavery', which meant that they had escaped from capture by a foreign ship

From 1536 until 1834, when the Poor Law Amendment Act changed the legal responsibility for the poor from parish to central government, the welfare of Piddlehinton's poor had been in the hands of the churchwardens, and from 1597, the overseers. The latter were appointed annually by two local JPs and had to be, in the words of the 1601 Act, 'substantial householders'. In such a poor community as Piddlehinton few people were willing to accept the unpaid and time-consuming job. In the seventeenth and eighteenth centuries the only substantial householder was the tenant of the desmesne farm. One of these was Nicholas Kellaway, whose 1783 will contained a clause allowing for £20 to be invested, the interest on which was to be paid to six poor widows of the parish at Christmas each year. In fact £12. 6s. 6d. only was paid by the executors on behalf of this charity, his effects being insufficient to pay the full amount. In 1923 the newly formed PCC took on the 'Kellaway Dole' and agreed to invest £13 in war loans, with surplus savings being handed to PCC accounts. The last time the Kellaway Dole appears to have been paid was 1934.

In 1620, of forty-eight householders, sixteen were paupers. These cottagers were known as the 'First Poor' because they were totally destitute and claimed from the poor rate. Labourers and servants were classed as the 'Second Poor' because they claimed occasional poor relief. The 1601 Act empowered the overseers to raise a compulsory weekly tax from those able to pay, including the rector. This was used, not only to give the poor money to spend, but also to buy raw materials to give them work, to pay for medical help, to apprentice children, and to build cottages for the homeless on waste ground. The Poorhouse in Piddlehinton, in London Row, was rebuilt in 1749.

Chapter 5

PIDDLEHINTON SCHOOL

The earliest reference to education in the village is an entry in the parish register of April 1755, relating to the payment of 12s. for one year's schooling for Symond Winser. This probably means board and lodging rather than education. Reference to a day school is made by the National Society for Promoting the Education of the Poor in the Principles of the Established Church, in the records of 1833, which reported three daily schools containing collectively thirty-two young children whose instruction was paid for by their parents. The 1846 General Church School Enquiry revealed sixty-two children attending day and Sunday schools in the village, and at that time there were three paid teachers.

In 1859, George Francis Coke, the curate of Piddlehinton, wrote to the National Society requesting them 'to give assistance in building a School, and in supporting it in a very poor parish'. A balance sheet was also sent as part of the application for a grant of £20. Out of a total cost of £429. 11s., the village raised £187. 7s. Eton College gave the site for the school building to the churchwardens.

The new school opened to pupils during 1861. The *County Chronicle* reported on 30 October, 'an excellent spread, provided for the school children by Rev. Coke, of tea and plum cake, served in the new school room after which they adjourned to the Rectory to play games'. However, the official opening – originally planned for 19 December 1861, but cancelled owing to the death of the Prince Consort – took place on 1 January 1862. The *County Chronicle* reported:

> The ceremony of opening the commodious new school took place on New Years Day and the proceedings created considerable interest among the parishioners by whom an anxious desire has long been felt to improve the accommodation afforded for the education of the rising generation of the humbler classes. The old school house was a dilapidated old place some little distance up the village . . .

The earliest school records available date from 1894 when there were eighty-eight children on the register – thirty boys and

Piddlehinton schoolhouse in 1904. Left to right: Miss Way, Miss Green (headmistress), Miss Myra Smith and Kate Ellis. High educational standards were obtained with Diocesan prizes being awarded to Kate Ellis, Alice and Ada Churchill and Kate Way, a record unequalled by any school in the Diocese.
▽

fifty-eight girls. In 1881 the Rev. Roper wrote to the National Society requesting assistance to build an extra classroom for forty-two children, as follows:

> We have between 70 and 80 children in our school and amongst them several infants for whom a gallery needs to be used in the one room with the older children. The want of a classroom is a great hindrance to the work of our schools but the interest in education is so slack in our little country village (with a population of about 400, no resident squire) and means are generally so inadequate that there is no hope of raising a sufficient sum or of obtaining any but very small subscriptions to the work amongst ourselves. The school was built (with aid from your Society) about 18 years since. Since that time our churchyard has been enlarged, our Church also enlarged and restored, the Rectory House enlarged and considerably improved so that for any new work our resources are at the lowest ebb.

In January 1890, a grant of £14 was made towards a total cost of £94. 2s. for enlarging the school. This must have been the infants' classroom where the gallery remained in use until 1906.

At the turn of the century, when less than thirty-five children attended, it was considered an insufficient number and the school was closed for the day. A number of children had to walk considerable distances to school, and when the weather was bad, there were frequent low attendances resulting in the closure of the school.

However, on the whole, the school seems to have had a good attendance record. In July 1901, Salisbury Diocesan medals were presented to seven pupils for full attendance during the year. In March 1898, two pupil teachers, Kate Ellis and Kate Way, took the

▷
Primrose Day in 1903. This is the earliest school photograph and shows the children wearing primroses in their buttonholes. Empire Day was also a favourite celebration enjoyed by the children, who dressed up to represent the colonies. They sang patriotic songs and took part in country dancing

first and second Diocesan prizes. Kate Way obtained a post as
assistant mistress at North Holwood near Dorking. A considerable
number of pupils went on to Teacher Training College.

Pupils at the school in 1909

Lessons throughout the school's lifetime were varied and included
knitting, needlework and cookery. The only mention of the 1914–18
war in school records is in September 1917, when children were
given time during the afternoons to pick blackberries for the
Ministry of Food. A total weight of 2209½ lb. of blackberries were
picked.

The school had a wide variety of teachers during its lifetime and in
1896 Miss Haywood came to the village from Whitelands College,
Chelsea. She had previously been a pupil teacher in a mixed village
school and was very fond of the country. Miss Haywood's sister
came with her, and they were both very keen to be involved in
village activities. In 1899, a night or continuation school for girls was
proposed, for girls who had left school at an early age and were in
danger of forgetting what they had learned.

It is difficult to trace the history of the school between 1926 and
1959 except from photographs supplied by local people as school
records for this period were destroyed. However, it is evident that
village life was very much influenced by school activities.

△
The school in 1930. The pupils are, from left to right; **Back row**, Sam Teversham, Ted Jeanes, Percy Teversham, Geoffrey Rendell, Denis Cheeseman, David Read. **Middle row**, Lily Gregory, Nellie Ford, Millicent ?, Kathleen Croft, Margaret Jeanes. **Front row**, Vera Hawkins, Teddy Cuff, Joyce Hawkins, Charlie Gregory, Margaret Vincent, Everett House, Violet Teversham

▷
The school in 1930. The pupils include Jack Way, Jack Gerrard, Jack Roberts, Ken Russell, Arthur Hatcher, Fred Hawkins, Nellie Roberts, Barbara Dyke, Lily Hawkins, Betty Joyce, Vera Vincent, Bob Read, Keith Hatcher, Winnie Murphy, Muriel Dyke, Winnie Hatcher and Reg Cosh

△   Piddlehinton school in 1937. The pupils are, from left to right; **Back row**, first on left?, Edna Churchill, Eileen Murphy, Fred Wills, Rene Trevett, Violet Teversham, Gordon Churchill, Kit Teversham, Ted Jeanes, Joan Taylor, Charlie Damen, Vera Hawkins, Joyce Southerns, Pat Trevett, Ruby Mans. **Middle row**, Betty Gregory, Sylvia Teversham, Mary Roberts, Iris Read, Fay Jeanes, Cynthia Read, Dorothy Trevett, ? Churchill, Linda Damen, Nigel Murphy, Terry Jeanes, John Maidment, Arthur Trevett, Stella Croft, Joan Murphy, Kitt Wills, Rose Wills. **Front row**, Bob Head, ?, Ralph Teversham, Norman Murphy, Richard Hansford, Bill Park, ? Churchill, David Moyson, George Damen, Ken Bartlett, Eddie Cosh. The teachers are Miss Way and Mrs Moyson

◁
The village school was closed in July 1981. At the final evening, Mrs Emily Hansford (née Woodland), the oldest village resident and a former pupil of the school, was presented with a bouquet

In 1981 the school was closed because numbers had declined, and the facilities were no longer up to modern standards. It was then that Piddlehinton children started going to the Piddle Valley First School in Piddletrenthide. Mr Billinge was the last headmaster, and Mrs Pickett, the assistant teacher.

Memories of Piddlehinton School in the 1920s and 1930s by Vera Vincent, a former pupil

The things I can remember most vividly are: our teacher – Miss Way – taking us out in the playground to see the occasional aeroplane in the sky! Trundling our hoops from home at Muston to School, and back – hanging them on the pegs in the school porch. Girls had wooden ones and the boys iron ones, made by the village blacksmith – Mr Fred Way. We would often watch him at work shoeing horses, making shoes, etc.

It was a wonderful experience to see a car on the road (as there were so few about), and we could hear it coming long before it reached us as it would be travelling quite slowly. When the Rev. Newman had his car in the 1920s, it was always a special pleasure for us to wave excitedly to him.

At one time, we used to push a tin lid along the road with a stick, and aim to get to school without making a hole in it.

Sunday school was held in church in the mornings – before the 11 a.m. service – and again in the afternoons. When it was cold weather, whilst waiting for the morning service to start, we would stand around the massive iron stove just inside the church door, to try to warm ourselves. But it certainly wasn't adequate heating for the whole church! Children were expected to go to Sunday school in both the morning and afternoon, but as we lived at Muston, once a Sunday was permissible for us. In the afternoons we waited at the Rectory for the Rev. and Mrs Newman and it was a rush to see who could be the lucky ones to hold one of their hands on the short journey to church.

We had Sunday school outings once a year to Weymouth – by charabanc in the early days until there were buses! We used to sing songs most of the way to Weymouth and back, but we weren't allowed to sing while passing through Dorchester. On our arrival at Weymouth, each child was given a sixpenny piece to spend! There was a Woolworths in Weymouth where everything was either 6d. or 3d.

After church on Christmas morning each child would be given an orange. On the day war was declared – Sunday 3 September 1939 – the congregation walked to the Rectory and heard the announcement on the wireless. Then everyone went back to church to continue the usual morning service. War had begun.

Mary Hardy and Kate Hardy

At the time Mary took up her teaching appointment at Piddlehinton, Thomas Hardy had also returned to the family home and having had a close relationship with his sister all his life, it is possible he would have accompanied her on many occasions on her journey to school. On the way they would have passed the manor at Waterston, purported to be Weatherbury Farm in his novel *Far From the Madding Crowd*, in which he used Mary as his model for Bathsheba Everdene.

Mary was a plain woman with a quiet nature and few friends, confiding in the first Mrs Thomas Hardy, 'nobody asks me to dinner or treats me like a lady'. This quiet temperament is possibly what endeared her to her brother Thomas, who was of a similar disposition.

It is thought that at some time during the 1870s, Mary actually lived in the schoolhouse at Piddlehinton, as Thomas Hardy is said to have brought his manuscripts to the schoolhouse for his sister to read before publication.

△
Mary Hardy, sister of the Dorset writer Thomas Hardy, taught in Piddlehinton school for several years from 1870. Born in 1852, she trained as a teacher at Salisbury and after teaching in Berkshire and Minterne Magna, Dorset, she returned home to Bockhampton and became headmistress at Piddlehinton

△
Mary Hardy's sketch of Piddlehinton Down from the school in 1872. Piddlehinton and the surrounding villages feature very prominently in a number of Thomas Hardy's novels and poems, in which reference is made to 'Longpuddle', which is thought to describe the Piddle Valley

△
Mary's younger sister Kate was a pupil teacher in Piddlehinton school prior to going to the same Diocesan Training College as Mary in 1877

Sunday School

As in most villages, considerable emphasis was placed on attendance at Sunday school, and village records show that in 1846 more children attended Sunday school than day school. At this time there were three teachers recorded. The rector wrote in the *Parish Magazine* that it was more important for local children to attend Sunday school than day school. Attendances were very good. The children were regularly invited to tea at the Rectory and on village outings as a reward.

In September 1896, the *Parish Magazine* urged parents to send their children to Sunday school, reminding them of their duty to see that children over the age of three years should be thoroughly instructed in 'the faith once delivered to the Saints'.

The same magazine reported that the rector's wife proposed opening a night school for young men and lads, through the winter. This would consist of classes in the schoolroom twice a week from 7.30 p.m. to 8.30 p.m. Members would be charged a penny a night for the lights and fuel, and during that one hour everybody would work hard. Eventually this class took place on Sunday afternoons at the Rectory, with six young lads present. The Sunday school continued until the early 1970s.

△
The old school building now in use as the Village Hall

From Village School to Village Hall

A fund to provide a village hall in Piddlehinton was started in 1925, with a balance of £19. 15s. 1d. from money collected for the War Memorial. It was decided to continue to press for a village hall as the need for a hall was very apparent. By 1980, fund raising had increased the amount to £2349, and it was in that year that the announcement came that the village school was to close. It was unanimously agreed that every effort should be made to raise the necessary money to purchase the building.

Various grants were provided and the old school was bought. Its conversion to the hall was completed in November 1982, and it was officially opened in April 1983. The hall is now in continuous use.

Chapter 6

VILLAGE BUSINESSES

The community of Piddlehinton was almost completely self-sufficient until the nineteenth century. Most of the occupations of village folk were directly or indirectly concerned with farming. Other employment reflected the changing pattern of village life. The earliest information which gives some insight into the standard of living of the Piddlehinton community is obtained from probate inventories of the more wealthy residents between the years 1664 and 1778. Fourteen such lists of personal property exist. Of these residents, seven were farmers. The average value of house contents, £26. 16s. 3d., is an extremely low figure for that time. The community was impoverished, with a great divide between the top five and the remaining nine residents listed.

In the latter half of the nineteeth century there were farmers (yeomen), a bailiff, carters, ploughmen, shepherds, dairymen and maids, agricultural engine drivers and many general agricultural labourers. Craftsmen and manufacturers included boot and shoemakers, a cordwainer, button makers, a saddler and harness maker, a tailor and tailoresses, seamstresses and dressmakers, a straw milliner, mop makers, glove makers, a twine spinner, a basket maker, thatchers, woodmen, hurdlers, spar makers, masons and bricklayers, plasterers, carpenters and blacksmiths.

Many residents provided services – bakers, millers, innkeepers and brewers, shopkeepers, butchers, a chimney sweep, laundresses, nurses, a nursemaid and a midwife, school mistresses and governesses, policemen, rectors, coachmen and a footman, ladies-, parlour-, house- and kitchen-maids, housekeepers, gardeners and cooks. There was a Major General along with Chelsea pensioners and a pensioner from the R&D Guards. Fund holders, an office clerk, land agents, a registrar of births and deaths, a tax collector, a printer compositor, annuitants and proprietors are also listed.

In 1851, eighty-nine households constituted a total population of 391. Of these, 288 people were aged 10 or over; 128 residents were involved in farming occupations, thirty-eight in crafts or manufacturing, and fifty-eight in services.

The Village Stores and Shopkeepers

In the 1841 census, William Purchase, Edmund Caundle, Ann Caddy and Joseph Cross are listed as shopkeepers. In 1851, Thomas Trimm and Ann Caddy are listed as grocers; Joseph Cross, Elizabeth and John Prior as grocery dealers; and Alfred Squire as shopman. By 1855, Miss Elizabeth Beck, Joseph Cross and George Tuck are shopkeepers. In 1859 and 1865, Louisa Loveless is a shopkeeper. Mrs Mary Cross replaces her husband from 1859 until 1871. In 1871 Daniel Baker is a licensed hawker and Amelia Tuck is helping her father, George, to run his grocery. By 1875, Mrs Mary Ann Tuck has taken over the store and continued to run it at least until 1885. In 1881, Frederick Vincent is a general dealer of a marine store, and Daniel Baker is still a hawker.

The year before (1880), a 37-year-old widow, Mary Rose, came to the village shop and post office. She had six young daughters to look after and bring up on her own – Florence 12, Mary 10, Helena 6, Ada 3, Annie 1, and a baby, Beatrice. She gave up the post office by 1903 but continued to run the shop at least until 1911. Her elder son, George, had been away working as a jockey. He came back to look after his mother and manage the grocery store, presently called Lantern Cottage, with his wife Mary (née Riggs), around 1915.

David Ellis and his wife kept the post office in the High Street at the corner of Folly Lane. This was one of the thatched houses burnt in 1933. David Ellis served as parish clerk from 1896 to 1926. He died in 1933, aged 91 years
▽

△   ▷
Fred and Mabel Gerrard kept the Piddlehinton village shop at Lantern Cottage from
1920 to 1952. They took over the Post Office when David Ellis retired

◁△   △
Fred and Mabel Gerrard's only son Jack joined the Royal Navy and served for twelve
years including the duration of the Second World War. The photograph (on the left)
shows Jack sitting on the steps of Mrs Dyke's cottage with Reg Yeatman. In 1941, Jack
married Wyn Riggs at Piddlehinton church. Jack has since died but Wyn still lives in
the village. The photographs of Jack and Wyn were taken after their wedding

Wyn Riggs' father, Bill Riggs, came to Piddlehinton from Chine Hill. He married Mrs Alice Hoskins, the postman's widow living in High Street. This photograph of the family was taken outside their cottage near the New Inn
▽

△ From 1952, Arthur and Gwen Billen ran the village shop and post office from the front room of Mr and Mrs Bob Gregory's thatched cottage, next to the bridge. They lived at Muston

△ In the late 1950s the Billens bought Lantern Cottage and the attached house from Eton College, for £400, and built the new post office and stores in the garden

Extra supplies could be obtained from representatives of Dorchester stores – Boons, Parsons and Wrights – or from Puddletown stores, who called to take orders which were delivered by van. Bakers and butchers came from Piddletrenthide. For those with a telephone, a call could be made to several Dorchester stores which would put the goods, including anything from fresh fish wrapped in newspaper to a pound of nails, on the bus to be sent out to the village.

The Drake family are remembered by many residents of Piddlehinton. Misses Suzie and Louie Drake and their brother Dickie had a sweet shop (which also sold a few groceries) in the High Street. Their mother, Elizabeth, had kept the shop before them between at least 1889 and 1920. It had a half door and a loud bell. They were all born in the village (Louisa 1873, Richard 1874, Susan 1876), and kept the shop until the 1940s. The sisters were very quaint and dressed in long black skirts and shawls. Dickie was a fine bricklayer and stonemason. He once walked, working all the way, from Piddlehinton to Scotland. They are remembered for their funny sayings. Dickie always pulled his wheelbarrow, 'because he couldn't stand the sight of it'. A favourite saying of Suzie's, when asked how she was, 'I du no I be down d ground and bide there'. She would also say, 'I spose tis true. I dun no if t'll stand movin.'

The New Inn, Innkeepers and Brewers

In medieval times the church was used as a parish hall. Ale, brewed on the premises and sold for church funds, was often drunk during dances and fairs held in the churchyard. One of the duties of the churchwardens was to organize 'Church Ales' – rural festivals where

◁
The consequence of sampling the local brew at the New Inn!

△

Mrs Caddy outside the New Inn c. 1900. Other known licencees and beer retailers from 1841 to 1923 include Benjamin Caddy, Richard Smith, George Groves, Mary Smith, Thomas Lovell, Mary Lovell, Giles Cross, Robert Pomeroy, Reuben Caddy, George Damen, Benjamin Gillingham, Mr Williams and F. Hawkins

▷

The New Inn c. 1930. Mrs Joyce Clare, Mr Hawkins' daughter, recalls the stairs to the first floor of the inn were opposite the entrance. To the left was the smoking room, with dartboard and shove ha'penny board. To the right was the public bar. The kitchen door opened on to the High Street

ale was consumed. Alcohol provided the main means of enlivening the dullness of village life!

Inventories from the seventeenth and eighteenth centuries survive, which reveal that private households often brewed ale or made cider on a small scale. On the tithe map, many orchards survived. One so-called 'yeoman' turned to larger-scale brewing as a means of supplementing his income. The New Inn was probably built in the late eighteenth century. Messrs Hall & Woodhouse of Blandford acquired the premises in 1898. The inn was described as, 'of mud, brick and flint construction with a thatched roof'. Outbuildings consisted of a stable for two horses, a small coach house, a cowshed and piggery, together with a well, stream, garden and orchard. As the only inn in Piddlehinton it provided (and still does) a focus for much of the social life of the villagers and visiting travellers.

Amongst the village characters using the inn was shopkeeper and mason, Mr Dickie Drake. Suffering from toothache but fearing the dentist, Mr Drake prevailed upon landlord Hawkins to pull out the offending tooth. This was duly accomplished but 'not until sufficient whisky had been consumed to give them both strength!'

The final landlords for Hall & Woodhouse were R. J. Waldon, Albert Penny, John Somers, Neville Anderson, Philip Legg and Andrew Hunt. The inn was renamed The Thimble in 1965. It was sold by the brewery in 1988 and is now a Free House.

At the time when Victorian society became concerned about the increased drinking in public houses, the Temperance Movement was formed seeking to persuade people to 'sign the pledge' and totally abstain from alcoholic drinks. Moderate drinkers were accepted as supporters, and a youth movement, the Band of Hope, was formed. The *Pyddle Hinton Parish Magazines* of 1896–1899 show that the movement was thriving, supported by local clergy.

Thomas and Elizabeth Squire, pictured here in 1869, came to Piddlehinton before 1818. They lived opposite the New Inn and most of their nine children were born in the village. In anger, Thomas Squire once threw a mallet at his son, Thomas Hall, who consequently left for London! Thomas and Elizabeth now rest side by side in the churchyard

Richard Lockett, the local master saddler and harness maker, married Louisa Squire. This picture dates from c. 1870. He was parish clerk and sexton for the last 20 years of his life. Richard and Louisa's daughter, Thirza, married the village shoemaker Tom Hardy in 1878

Henrietta Squire, another daughter of Thomas and Elizabeth, lived with Richard and Louisa Lockett. Henrietta worked in the village as a tailoress and was very good at her trade

Charles Squire, one of the sons of Thomas and Elizabeth, was a shoemaker. He had married by 1841 and moved away shortly afterwards

The Smith family lived at Waterfall Cottage, next to the old mill, from the 1850s until it burnt down in 1925. Frederick (b. 1856) was the son of gardener Richard Smith and his wife Harriet, a laundress. He had been apprenticed to a carpenter in Dorchester and married Amelia, daughter of local grocer and thatcher George Tuck. They had nine children. Fred, with sons Dick and George, ran their workshop as coachbuilders, carpenters, wheelwrights, joiners and undertakers, on the site of the old mill. This photograph shows Fred, Dick and George in the mill garden

△

The Smiths made coffins in competition with the Saint family. Evelyn Smith married gardener Charlie Jeanes and continued to live in the family home until their daughter, Margaret, was three. This picture shows Evelyn in 1912. She lined the coffins with pitch and made pillows of sawdust

△

Fred Smith died in 1934. Dick Smith carried on as a craftsman carpenter. He even made and played his own violin. He often cut the villagers' hair in the carpenter's shop. Bill Smith (pictured here) later joined the business to help out

△

The Saint family came to Piddlehinton before 1895. Henry Saint was followed by Douglas Saint in 1911, and Albert Saint in 1920. From No. 4 High Street Bert Saint ran a carpenter's and undertaker's business. On funeral days he pushed the coffins to church on a hand cart, always wearing his top hat. The photograph shows Albert Saint and family

△

Albert Saint married a local girl, Mabel Jeanes. Their only son Wilfred, who used to help make the coffins, still lives and works in the village. The picture shows Mabel with Wilf as a baby

Carpenters

Four families of carpenters, the Squires, Smiths, Saints and Gales, are worthy of special attention.

On the site of the present village shop and post office, John Gale ran a carpenter's and wagonmaker's workshop from 1911 onwards. John Gale was born in Powerstock, moved to Cheselbourne, then Muston and later to Piddlehinton.

His eleventh child was named 'Dolly'. Her sister Bessie, who had called her 'my very own live Dolly', died of pneumonia at the age of five years. The family perpetuated the pet name, although she had been baptized Alice. At the age of sixteen, Dolly took up a position as personal maid and companion to Emma (first wife of author Thomas Hardy) in the last year of Mrs Hardy's life. Thomas Hardy and Dolly were the only two people present at Emma's bedside when she died. John and Fanny Gale had not wished Dolly to work in the household, as Thomas Hardy had a dubious reputation locally. Consequently, Dolly kept this episode in her life a secret. With the outbreak of the First World War, Dolly went into war work. In 1916, she met a young Canadian soldier Tom Harvey, whom she married.

After the war, they settled in Canada and shared forty-two happy years of marriage. Two of their six children were born in England.

Tom died in 1960. He never knew of Dolly's time with the Hardys as her story was only uncovered by the English press in the early 1970s, resulting in an article in the *Sunday Observer* on 14 May 1972. Now aged ninety-two, Dolly Gale Harvey still lives in Ingersoll, Canada.

Many of the Gale grandchildren were brought back to Piddlehinton to be baptized. Fanny, John, Bessie, Elsie and May all rest in Piddlehinton churchyard.

John Gale settled with his wife Fanny and their children, in the cottage next to Lantern Cottage. They had twelve children. The picture shows the Gale family *c.* 1908. They are Ethel, Harry, Elsie, Tom, Susie, Arthur, Eva, Dolly, John, Fanny, May and Walter
▽

△
Dolly Gale and Tom Harvey were married in Piddlehinton church on New Year's Day, 1918

▷
Arthur, Harry and Walter Gale were, at different times, apprenticed in the family business. The three eldest sons went to Canada adventuring before the First World War. Tom is seen here working on the Canadian Pacific Railway, before joining the Canadian Army with Harry and Arthur

John Way's son Fred also followed the family tradition. The smithy was always a great fascination to villagers. There was always someone looking over the half door watching the horses being shod

Blacksmiths

Five generations of the Way family ran the blacksmith's forge in the High Street from the 1830s until the 1940s. George Way was born in Tolpuddle in 1799. He brought his wife and three children from Puddletown (where their youngest son James was born in 1827) to settle in Piddlehinton. As a master blacksmith, George employed two hands. James Way became a blacksmith journeyman, and at least two of his five sons, John and Alfred, entered the family trade. John was apprenticed in 1871, aged fifteen, and presumably took on the responsibility of the village forge on the death of his grandfather George on 10 March 1874. Alfred became a blacksmith journeyman like his father (as mentioned in the 1881 census, aged seventeen).

John and his wife Emma also had three daughters who all became pupil teachers at Piddlehinton school at the turn of the century, and went on to train as teachers. Rose Way returned to Piddlehinton school as assistant teacher in 1907, teaching the infant class. As the church organist for twenty-nine years she helped to train the choir and taught local children to play the piano. She played a very active part in village life. John Way died in December 1937.

The blacksmith's forge, opposite the mill in the High Street, has recently been converted into a private garage

Fred Way's son Bill, outside the old forge in the 1930s

◁

Another of Fred's sons, Jack, became the last blacksmith in the village. Fewer horses were kept as the farms became mechanized in the 1940s. Jack Way adapted his business to work on cars. Some of the family still live locally

Milling and Millers at the Manor Corn Mill

First references to the watermill in Piddlehinton are found in 1440, 1462 and 1571. By the sixteenth century, it is clear that it was the grist mill for the Manor of Piddlehinton. The Tithe Apportionment of 1838 shows William Moores occupying 'a House, Mill, Stable and Garden'. In May 1841, William Moores insured 'the stock and utensils of his windmill and bakehouse (including cloths for the mill sails and three pairs of millstones)' for £60 with the Sun Insurance Co. This is a puzzle as there seems no logical explanation for any windmill in a valley, and no stone foundations remain. It would have been an unusual departure from Dorset custom. No mention of a windmill is found either before or after this one, except for the windmill (windpump) near East Farm buildings, later, in the twentieth century. A bakehouse was evidently on the premises. Other Piddlehinton millers included Katherine Lowman, George White, Charles Moores, James Guy and Edward Chilcott.

In the late 1860s, James Clarke from Affpuddle came to Piddlehinton to take over the corn mill. He employed Andrew Gregory as miller's boy in 1871. A master miller, James Clarke was married with four children. He died aged forty in 1874, leaving his wife, Caroline, to carry on the business until 1890. She employed one man to help her. No reference to a miller is found by 1898.

Sometime soon after this, the mill workings were dismantled. The wheel of the mill had been removed before the early years of the twentieth century, when Mr Frederick Smith and his sons worked on the site as wheelwrights, carpenters, joiners and also undertakers. The mill cottage, 'Waterfall', burnt down in 1925 (see page 85).

△
Only one wall of the mill remains. This has a stone pentrough which would have delivered the water to the millwheel. The last millwheel in use was breast-shot, and operated by water falling by gravity into the higher wheel buckets, and dropping out at the bottom – the weight rather than the velocity of the incoming water turning the wheel. The end of the leat, near the mill, is now dry but can still be traced

◁
One millstone of Derbyshire Peak stone (Millstone grit), used for coarse grinding, still remains

Thatching

George Hansford and Jack Osgood thatching together in Plush, in 1969. George Hansford was a master thatcher in Piddlehinton for about fifty years. When he first arrived in 1928, there were four other thatchers in the Piddle Valley. During his time he thatched most of the thatched houses in the valley. He was awarded three certificates for his skills and one for teaching. He trained seven apprentices including Jack Osgood, the only thatcher still to live in the valley. Jack married June Croft who lived at West Lodge Cottages ▽

Several residents were employed as thatchers or in the related occupations of spar making, hurdling, or as woodmen. They include Jacob Tuck (1841), John Paine, Joseph Groves, Thomas and George Tuck (1851), George Groves, Thomas, George and John Tuck (1861), Thomas and John Jeanes, Richard Foot, John Drake, Alfred and George Groves (1881).

The farms employed local thatchers at harvest time. Before the corn was threshed, the sheaves were stored in thatched ricks. Three months later, the thatch was removed and the dry corn threshed. The straw was then stored in newly thatched ricks. All hay ricks were also thatched. The preparation of hazel and withy spars, and also house thatching, provided employment for the remainder of the year. During the war years, house thatching was not permitted. The massive effort to grow corn in the Second World War resulted in forty-one barley ricks being thatched on Bourne Farm in a single year. Rick thatching declined with the arrival of the combine harvester.

The Boot-repairer

Ambrose Brown was a boot-repairer who lived and worked in the High Street next to the blacksmith's cottage. He was often called 'Dad' Brown, with affection and he used to give the village children apples from his garden. This story is told of Ambrose Brown:

Mrs Ellen Trevett was an old lady who used to lay out the dead and bring in the babies. One day the late Mrs Lovelace met her in Piddlehinton High Street and asked her:

'Where are you going, Mrs Trevett?'

'I've got to go up to Ambrose Brown's,' she answered. 'He've died.'

Soon afterwards, Mrs Lovelace was looking out of the window of her house and saw Mrs Trevett coming back.

'You've been quick,' she said.

'Well,' Mrs Trevett told her, 'I went up to Ambrose Brown's and turned back the sheet off his face and he said: "What be you come vor, Mrs Trevett? I 'aven't 'ad me breakfast yet!"'

Sadly, Mr Brown did in fact die a few days later.

△
Hermann Lea took this photograph of Ambrose Brown the boot-repairer in 1899, when Ambrose was working for John Antell at Puddletown, before his time in Piddlehinton

Joey Hardy

Another resident in the early part of this century, remembered by many, was Joey Hardy. He lived in the house next to the river, now known as 'Bridge House'. There were no curtains at the windows and a candle could be seen burning on his table when the village children peeped in. He would often tease them and buy them sweets. His son had been killed in the First World War and he lived alone. For income he relied on selling wild flowers and rabbits at the market. He picked bunches of sweet violets from the hedgerows and has become a legendary figure for his association with snowdrops. Once each year, he would take his seat in church, always at the time that snowdrops were in flower. Parson Newman would see him in the congregation and expect him at the Rectory door a day or so afterwards! Sure enough he would call round and ask if he might pick some snowdrops from the Rectory garden. The rector would always oblige and Joey Hardy would take them to Dorchester to sell. In Piddlehinton church we now celebrate Snowdrop Sunday each February in commemoration.

Chapter 7

SOME PIDDLEHINTON PEOPLE

The census records show that there are a few families who came to the village before 1841, and still have descendants living here. These are the Coshes, Jeanes, Lovelaces and Ways. The Churchills had the longest connection of all, until they sold Muston in 1976. Other families have been in the village for more than one generation including the Belgraves, Damens, Dykes, Gerrards, Gregorys, Greens, Hansfords, Murphys, Reids, Riggs, Saints and Torys. There are also records of others who lived in the village in earlier times, who led interesting lives. There must be many more. This chapter gives a few details of some of these families, in alphabetical order.

The Astell Family

Major and Mrs Astell bought West Lodge in 1862. They altered it extensively, adding a conservatory, leading to a new front door, on the east side of the house.

In 1871 the census records Major Astell JP and his Irish wife,

▷
The coach house at West Lodge which the Astells built in 1898 to celebrate their Golden Wedding. Its clock is the only striking one in the village

Harriette, living in the house with their son and four daughters, an American governess, a Swiss ladies'-maid, a parlour-maid, a housemaid and a kitchen-maid. The gardener and the coachman and their families lived in West Lodge Cottages. Mrs Astell was very eccentric and imported her own carefully chosen coffin from the Continent. She always liked to be known as Madam Astell. She was very interested in folklore.

In 1917 their only son, Godfrey, was killed in action in France, and after that they sold the house to Col. and Mrs Belgrave.

John Baverstock Knight

John Baverstock Knight was described in his obituary as, 'a magnificent specimen of a country squire, six foot in height, handsome, well dressed . . . full of country interests, stock, agriculture, apple culture; an excellent sportsman in hunting, shooting and fishing and professionally a land agent . . . further he was a churchwarden and notable for his charities . . . He had the reputation of a wit and a turn for scribbling letters in verse.' Added to this he was a skilled and prolific painter, having been encouraged by his father from his early youth.

Some of his etchings appear in *Hutchin's History of Dorset*, and his paintings are to be found in many museums including the British Museum and the Victoria and Albert Museum in London, and the Dorchester Museum.

In his professional capacity he was land agent to several local landowners. He was appointed Commissioner for the Piddlehinton Enclosure Act of 1835, supervising the transition from open down farming to the present field system.

In order to pursue this great range of activities, he had the habit of getting up at 5 a.m. and working at his art in his studio from 6 a.m. till 9 a.m. He would then devote the rest of the day to business, sport and leisure.

Unfortunately there are few records of his activities in the village. Even the records of the auction of over 300 of his paintings at West Lodge after his death in 1859 were destroyed by a fire at Ensor's, the auctioneers.

△
John Baverstock Knight, born in 1785 near Blandford, bought West Lodge in 1812 and lived there with his wife, Elinor, and a family of eight children for 47 years, until his death in 1859

◁
This oil painting by John Baverstock Knight is on the domed ceiling of his old studio at West Lodge. His works also include etchings, watercolours, portraits of many Dorset Families and copies of old masters

▷
Col. and Mrs John Belgrave bought West Lodge in 1917. Here Col. Belgrave DSO, Royal Artillery, on home leave from France, is seen with his wife Gwladys and their elder son Richard at West Lodge shortly after they bought it. Their younger son, Robert, was born there

△
The Belgraves' car outside West Lodge soon after they moved to the house in 1917

△
Tom Cosh and his wife Elizabeth. This photograph was taken during the 1914–18 war

The Belgrave Family

Colonel and Mrs Belgrave were interested in everything that took place in the village. Gwladys took the lead in establishing the Piddlehinton Women's Institute. Their annual Flower Show, an important village event, was held at West Lodge, as were the meetings of the Wolf Cub pack she started. She was very keen for the village to have a hall, and it was at her suggestion that the balance of the War Memorial Fund was used to start the Village Hall Fund. She died in 1937.

When Col. Belgrave retired from the army in 1932, he also took an active part in village life as churchwarden and school manager. He played a leading part in the formation of the Dorset branch of the Council for the Preservation of Rural England, and in the running of the British Legion. He invited all Piddlehinton ex-servicemen to an annual Armistice Day dinner at West Lodge.

In 1938 he was recalled to the army. On his second retirement in 1942, he joined the Dorset Home Guard, acting as Chief of Staff to its Commander, General Sir Henry Jackson of Piddletrenthide. He resumed his village activities and was well known in the village for the prize apples he grew and shared.

On his death in 1955, the house passed to his son Robert, who lives there now with his wife, Susan.

The Cosh Family

The Cosh family have been living in Piddlehinton since at least 1820. Tom Cosh (1891–1968) was quite a character. He worked on the farm for the Lovelaces for many years. He fought in the First World War, and served in the Home Guard in the Second World War. He was sexton for 30 years and there is a plaque to his memory in the church. His granddaughter and great-grandchildren live in the village.

The Dyke Family

△
Laura Dyke's eldest daughters, Mabel and Elsie, were nurses at Herrison Hospital, Charminster. They walked to work along the unmade road. This photograph was taken in 1909

Laura Dyke outside her cottage (now demolished) with granddaughter Fay. Two of Mrs Dyke's younger children, Edward and Gussie, went to sea. Her other daughter, Florrie, married local farmworker William Jeanes and they lived in Piddlehinton with their three children, Ted, Fay and Terry
▽

△
Laura Dyke in her garden on the corner of London Row and High Street overlooking Lantern Cottage. Her daughter, Mabel, married Fred Gerrard, and ran the Post Office and village stores at Lantern Cottage. The had one son, Jack

Elsie Dyke married her cousin Ern Yeatman and moved away to Surrey. They had two children; Reg, who was killed in the Second World War, and Laura, who often visited Piddlehinton, and now lives in the village
▽

△
Mrs Laura Dyke and her five children moved to Piddlehinton in 1908. In her early 40s and recently widowed, Laura helped Parson Newman with his house cows and worked for Miss Riggs at Manor Farmhouse, serving milk to the villagers

◁
Cyril Green married Christobel Chaldecott, whose parents farmed at White Lackington. Their first home was Myrtle Cottage, but they later moved to Bournemouth to run a shop. Two years later they came back to Piddlehinton to farm

The Green Family

Cyril Green, the son of a gamekeeper, was born in Kingrove House, Piddletrenthide. On leaving school, and being too young to enlist to fight in the war, he helped his father farm Hope Farm, Piddletrenthide.

Cyril and his wife rented The Laurels from Eton, and leased Kiddles Farm from Colonel Belgrave, and Higher Heave Farm, as sub-tenants, from Rex Lovelace. They took over Hope Farm and, eventually, White Lackington Farm. These farms totalled 600 acres, and animals and machinery were all moved between the different farms. Cyril employed local people. Percy Teversham was his dairyman, and Arthur King, Herbie Trevett and the younger Ivor Spracklen all worked for him.

They eventually bought The Laurels, making it a happy home; their children, Philip and Rosmond, were raised there. As well as running his farms, Cyril was both a Parish and a District Councillor, actively representing the community until shortly before his death in 1977.

△
Cyril, seen here talking to Barbara, one of the two land girls from London, who joined his workforce during the war. They are standing beside his Massey Harris combine

The Gregory Family

Bill Gregory was born at Black House, one of nine children. His family moved to Rectory Road when Bill was very young. Bill's mother was the local midwife and young Bill was pressed into service as a guide during darkness, holding a candle in a jam jar as a lantern to help her find her way to confinements.

His father worked for Mr Mayo at Little Piddle Farm. Among his duties were those of a drowner, maintaining the water meadows along the Piddle. Bill used to catch trout and eels which got stranded when the hatches were opened. Bill worked at Manor Farm for Mr and Miss Riggs until he was eighteen, when he became a bricklayer.

In 1939 Bill joined the LDV (later to become the Home Guard), where his skill as a bricklayer was put to good use. In 1942 he enlisted in the Royal Engineers and trained as a stevedore, working in the London docks. During the invasion of Normandy, he worked on the Mulberry Harbour, the floating harbour towed to Normandy and used to land supplies. When he left the army in 1945, he joined the Reserve. He was a very keen supporter of the British Legion for the rest of his life.

In 1941, when his mother died, Bill and his family moved into his parents' house in Rectory Road. His brother, Charlie, lived with them. Two other brothers, Leonard and Bob, also lived in the village with their families, but later moved away. Bill died in 1982, and Emily in 1988.

The Jeanes Family

The Jeanes family have lived in the village since John Jeanes arrived with his wife, Sarah, to work on the land. The census records show that this was before 1841. The Jeanes' holding in 1871 was of 41 acres, and two men and a boy were employed. They kept sheep and grew corn. The family lived at White's Dairy House and in the dairy cottages.

△
Bill and Emily Gregory celebrating their Golden Wedding. Bill married Emily Woodland in 1932 and they set up house at No. 14 High Street. Emily had come to the village in 1916 with her parents, when she was eight

◁
Haymaking was a family occasion. This nineteenth-century postcard was sent to 'Bess', showing Uncle Tom's family. 'Uncle Tom' was the elder Tom Jeanes. Ern Yeatman (marked) came from Surrey, but visited Aunt Laura Dyke and cousins, including Elsie Dyke whom he later married

△
Tom Jeanes Jnr was one of the last farming tenants of Eton. Born in 1894, he farmed about 90 acres with his uncle Tom Jeanes, as had his grandfather, William Jeanes, before him. He is seen here with village children including Wilf Saint, Jack Gerrard, Ted Jeanes and Doris and Alfred Barrett

△
Tom and Terry Jeanes at harvest time, August 1949. When his uncle, Tom Jeanes, died, Eton passed the tenancy down to Tom Jnr. Terry Jeanes and Joe Damen worked for him. He always kept a barrel of home-made cider in his barn by the churchyard 'for social pleasure'

△
Tom Jeanes, with Jack Gerrard on the horse. Many men and boys from the village spent time helping Tom on his farm, as in the days of Tom's uncle

△
Tom Jeanes retired in 1966, the end of the Eton era. He was the last copyhold farmer to farm in the village. This photo was taken in 1977. He died in 1978.

△
Tom Jeanes Jnr had two brothers, Walter and William, and five sisters. Sister Mabel married Albert Saint. Other sisters moved away. Walter was killed in the First World War. William (on the binder) returned to work for Captain Fellowes on Manor Farm. Herbie Downton is driving the tractor (c. 1949)

◁
William Jeanes and Florrie Dyke married in Piddlehinton church in 1920. Their twin children, Terry and Fay, still live in the village and both take an active part in village life. Terry is sexton, and a bellringer. Fay is married to Geoff Lord, the organist

▷
Ted, elder son of Bill and Florrie Jeanes, worked as a butcher for Wightmans in Piddletrenthide. He joined the navy during the Second World War. He died in 1965 leaving a family in Dorchester

The Lovelace Family

For five generations the Lovelace family have farmed in Piddlehinton. Joseph Lovelace's name first appears as a tenant of Eton College in 1817. In the Tithe Award of 1838, he is listed as farming five holdings, totalling 152 acres.

By the 1851 census, his son James, aged 31, is the farmer and

△
Walter Lovelace with his wife Millicent, their daughter Elneth and their son Rex. The photograph was taken at East Farm, about 1912. Walter, a churchwarden for many years, farmed until his death in 1927

◁
Rex Lovelace with his son Bill and John Randall their shepherd discussing their Dorset Down sheep. John Randall once won the Stockman of the Year title for the country

miller. Like his father, he frequently held office in the Manorial Court. By 1861, he and his wife Susan farmed 560 acres, and employed twenty men and eight boys. They had eight children, the youngest of whom, Walter, took on the tenancy on his father's death.

Walter's son, Rex, took over the farm as a young man, on his father's death. In 1942 he bought the 44 acres of Glebe land. After the Second World War, he also took over the tenancy of Manor Farm. He was for some years chairman of the South Dorset Hunt and chairman of the Piddlehinton Parish Council, until it merged with other parishes to form the Piddle Valley Parish Council in 1977. He died in 1978.

Rex's son, Bill, who took on the tenancy, died in 1981. His wife Jane exchanged the tenancy for the freehold of part of the property, which she still farms today.

Thomas Meggs (1736–1819)

Thomas Meggs was the tenant of Eton's Manor Farm for 33 years, from 1786 until his death in 1819. In 1794, aged 58, he joined the Dorset Volunteer Rangers, the newly formed force raised privately by Lord Milton, son of the Earl of Dorchester, to defend the county against invasion by Napoleon. They agreed to receive no pay, and to clothe and horse themselves, receiving only a sword and a pistol from the government. They undertook to attend for training not more than twice a week, and not during harvest or sheep shearing.

In 1797, when the danger of invasion increased, Lt Meggs became a captain and raised his own troop. The whole force numbered 380. It was reviewed by George III on Fordington Field in 1798, and again in 1799 and 1801. The king was 'highly pleased and gratified with the whole appearance and performance'. When peace was signed in 1802, the Dorset Volunteer Rangers were disbanded. They were the forerunners of the Dorset Yeomanry.

Thomas Meggs held office in the Manorial Court in Piddlehinton in 1816. There is a tablet in the church to his memory, and to that of his wife Susan, who died two weeks after her husband in 1819 and their only son, who died in 1821. There is also a tablet dedicated to the memory of their daughter, Susan Crewe.

△
This portrait of Capt. Thomas Meggs (1798), in the uniform of the Dorset Volunteer Rangers was painted by Thomas Beach, a leading portrait painter

PC 89, James Searley

PC James Searley was stationed at Piddlehinton from 1855 to 1888. He lived in a cottage in the village which also served as the Police Station. During the course of his duties, he had to travel miles to other towns and villages, all on foot. Only the superintendents in charge of divisions were required to provide themselves with a horse. It was not until 1894 that Dorchester Division acquired its first bicycle. James Searley was graded as a first-class constable, and his wages were £1. 3s. 4d. a week. A police officer lived in the village until 1926.

James Searley kept a very interesting journal, from which a few extracts follow:

1885
October 19th: Detected Harry Harwood stealing apples value 6d. the property of Mr James Lovelace of Piddlehinton.
Nov 9th: Special duty at Sherborne Election and returned to my station in the night.

1886
March 26th: Apprehended John Jones for begging alms at Piddlehinton and took him to Dorchester.
March 27th: Attended Petty Sessions to give evidence against John Jones for begging. Committed for 14 days hard labour.
June 3rd: Received a complaint from Mr J. Riggs of Piddlehinton that some person had cut off his cow's tail. Made immediate enquiries and examined cow and am of opinion that it was not cut off but suffering from tail worm. Reported the particulars to Superintendent Gale.

1887
April 30th: To Dorchester to report to Supt. Gale particulars of a fire at Piddlehinton on the same date destroying house and furniture the property of Albert Harding. Also did duty before and after the fire.
July 14th: Moved some gypsies from Waterston Ridge.
August 22: Served school attendance summons personally on George Woodward at Lower Waterston.
Nov 5th: Attended Petty Sessions to give evidence against George and William Larcombe for being drunk in charge of horses and furious driving, fined 30/- each including costs.

△
PC Frisby, the present Piddle Valley policeman, dressed in a uniform such as James Searley would have worn. He read extracts from PC 89's journal at the 'Evening of Village Entertainment', held the night before 'The Story of Piddlehinton' exhibition opened in March 1988

The Tory Family

Clement Tory bought Muston Manor in 1906. He never lived there but he farmed the land. On his death in 1940, two of his sons, Philip and Edgar, each bought parts of the estate. Philip married Nancy Lovelace, daughter of Walter Lovelace, and lived at Mullets, Piddletrenthide, farming here for a while before moving away.

Edgar bought Bourne Farm, to which he and his bride Freda moved in 1941. He later bought his brother's land adjoining it as well. Edgar and Freda farmed at Bourne for 23 years and raised their three daughters there.

In 1964 they sold Bourne Farm to Ingram Spencer of Hanford Farms, and moved to Higher Waterston, where they farmed a smaller acreage. Although then outside the parish boundary, they kept their connection with Piddlehinton. Edgar served as a church-warden from 1972 until his death in 1989. He was a keen sportsman and naturalist, and knew all the country round Piddlehinton 'like the back of his hand'.

▷
The wedding of Philip Tory and Nancy Lovelace. From left to right: Frank Tory, Rex Lovelace, Mrs Millicent Lovelace, Philip Tory, Nancy Lovelace, Eric Tory. Sitting are Elneth Lovelace and Enid Tory

△
Edgar and Freda Tory out with the South Dorset Hounds. He was a joint Master of the Hunt from 1965 to 1980

△
Edgar and Freda Tory with their three daughters at Bourne Farm

The Winzer Family

Ann Winzer tended the wounded at the battle of Waterloo, many years before Florence Nightingale pioneered the nursing of the sick and wounded in the Crimean War. Born in Dorchester, Ann came to live in Piddlehinton after her nursing days with the army were over. She married James Winzer, who was also born in Dorchester. He must have seen military service, probably overseas, for he was a Chelsea Pensioner though, like many others, he did not live at the Royal Hospital, Chelsea. It seems that Colonel Astell, who came to live in the village in 1862, took steps to ensure that she also got a pension in recognition of her service to the army.

In the 1871 census, James gives his profession as plasterer journeyman. Their son Joseph, born in 1844, followed the same profession.

The inscription on Ann Winzer's tombstone is as follows:

SACRED
TO
THE MEMORY OF
ANN
THE BELOVED WIFE OF
JAMES WINZER
WHO DEPARTED THIS LIFE ·
NOVEMBER 28TH 1873
AGED 82 YEARS
She was a Waterloo heroine
who assisted at that fam-
ous battle AD 1815 by aiding
& assisting the sick & wounded. She endured many hards-
hips having followed the
British army from Brussels
to Paris. From Paris to Duney.
Returned to England & from
thence to the Rock of Gibr-
altar where she remained
4 years. She afterwards re-
sided in this parish where
she received a pension through the instrumentality of
Colonel Astell with that of
many other officers by whose kindness this stone is
raised as a tribute of res-
pect to a long life spent
in true and faithful service.

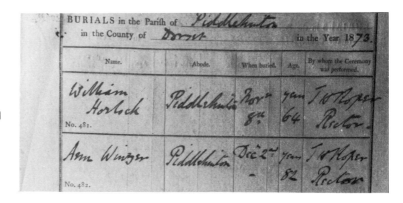

▷
The record of Ann Winzer's burial in 1873 from the register of Piddlehinton church. She is buried in the churchyard and her tombstone tells her story. Her husband died two years later

The Woodland Family

Frank Woodland came to Piddlehinton as a carter, working for Walter Lovelace. He had had a disagreement with his employer, Lady Debenham, of Briantspuddle, who required him to work on Sundays. Consequently, he sought a new position. He was too late for the annual February hiring fair in Dorchester for jobs starting in April, so he advertised his services in the *Western Gazette*. Walter Lovelace, farming at East Farm, Piddlehinton, came in a pony and trap to interview him and took him on as carter.

Mr and Mrs Woodland had eight children of whom Emily was the youngest. They lived at East Farm Cottages until Mr Woodland's retirement in 1931. Then they moved to a cottage in West Lane which is no longer standing. Emily attended the village school until she was fourteen, and then went into service in Puddletown as 'between maid', earning £12 a year. Later she worked as a housemaid in Tolpuddle earning £14.

In 1932 Emily married Bill Gregory, and they lived in Piddlehinton for the rest of their lives.

▷
Frank Woodland, carter to Walter Lovelace at East Farm from 1916 to 1931

Chapter 8

ORGANIZATIONS AND CELEBRATIONS

Over the years there have been many different groups and organizations in the village.

There are reports of a **cricket club** as far back as 1898. There have been several other cricket clubs over the years although there are no records. However, a cricket pitch is marked on some old maps in the field south of the Rectory.

Piddlehinton men have always loved **football**. It is certain that there was a team before the First World War and there is a report that it was re-formed in 1938. Since then, there has always been one in Piddlehinton.

△
Piddlehinton Football Team before the First World War. Some of the players are Charlie Dyke, Bill Smith, Walter Jeanes, Bill Jeanes, Fred Way, Alf Dyke and Jack Dyke

△
The Piddlehinton Football Team in 1949. Some of the players are Jack Way, Mr Davis, Ted Boardman, Ken Green, Wilf Saint, Don Wightman, Arthur Trevett, John Gregory and Jim Wills

Notice Their Knitting Needles

Sweet 20 and Wise 75 Unite In Dorset Village Industry

Puddlehinton Stockings Cross The Border—And Climb Mount Everest

PASS through Puddlehinton any day when a warm sun is shining, and you will probably see several women knitting at their doorways. They are members of the Puddlehinton Village Knitting Industry who have gained many awards at arts and crafts shows for the excellence of their work.

The industry is conducted by Mrs. Kenneth Churchill, wife of Comdr. K. B. M. Churchill, of Muston Manor, who conceived the idea 14 years ago. It was actually mooted at a meeting of the village Women's Institute but the industry has no connection with the Institute today. Mrs. Churchill has spent many years in Scotland and she told an "Echo" reporter this week how villagers in the most remote villages of Scotland knit stockings and take them to the social gatherings held in the autumn for sale.

COSTS THEM NOTHING

"I thought it would be a good idea if something on those lines could be introduced at Puddlehinton," said Mrs. Churchill. "It costs the women of the village nothing. I buy the wool and they make the stockings, and we sell them for just enough to pay for the wool and leave a little over for the knitters themselves. Hundreds of stockings have been made in Puddlehinton since we started and we have sent them to all parts of the world."

When I called at Muston Manor, writes the reporter, Mrs. Churchill was busily engaged in packing stockings which had been ordered. They were chiefly golf and snooting stockings, beautifully and very strongly made. Mrs Churchill keeps a record of where the stockings go, and strangely enough, although stockings are made by the thousand in Scotland, she has many orders from across the border.

YOUNGEST, OLDEST

Miss Phyllis Riggs, 20 years old, is the youngest member of the Puddlehinton knitting industry. Seventy-five years old Mrs. T. Read, senior, whose picture you see on this page, is the oldest. Despite her age Mrs. Read secured a certificate for her work at the recent arts and crafts show at Canford and she possesses two other first-class certificates as well as a second and other awards, all for stockings and socks.

"I should feel lost if I hadn't my

knitting to do," said Mrs. Read as her clever fingers manipulated the needles. "After I have done my housework and sewing I always start straight away on my knitting. I never miss a day."

UP MOUNT EVEREST

Mrs. Read is exceptionally proud of the fact that at one exhibition the Duchess of Athlone bought a pair of stockings for the Duke and that another pair of stockings from her needles were worn by Mr. Tom Brocklebank, of Fontwell Magna, when he was a member of the 1933 Mount Everest expedition. Another pair was given by Mr. Brocklebank to the porter who is claimed to have reached a higher point on the mountain than any living man.

△

The Dorset Daily Echo, 29 April 1939

▷

The Women's Institute sock knitting group. They are Mrs Churchill, Mrs Newman, Miss Gerrard, Mrs Saint, Mrs Millicent Lovelace, Mrs Bill Jeanes, Mrs Bagg, Mrs Bob Gregory, Mrs Bill Gregory and Mrs Reid

For many years there was a lively **Women's Institute**. It ran from 1918 to 1969. In 1918 Mrs Gwladys Belgrave took the lead in forming the first Women's Institute in Piddlehinton. Excerpts from the records include:

1919 the ladies became interested in rush-work classes, learning to make baskets and mats. Dozens of men's working baskets and many mats were made. Classes were held at West Lodge. At an exhibition held in London, Mrs Cornick, one of the oldest members, was awarded a gold medal. The medal hung in a frame in the school.

1921 it was arranged to have a gypsy picnic with music at West Lodge.

1926 it was planned to enter a singing competition. The first test was held in the Corn Exchange, Dorchester. The little choir did well and secured 182 marks out of 200, beating many other village WIs. As a result they were sent to the Pavilion, Weymouth, for the final where they scored over 180. The choir was trained by Miss Way, and the accompanist was Mrs Belgrave. This year also, Mrs Churchill of Muston formed a knitting committee and quite an industry was developed knitting socks.

Starting in 1933, annual summer flower shows were held at West Lodge. The show in 1939 had to be cancelled because of the war. With the coming of the Second World War the WI members became very active. In 1940 they had a sale in aid of the Dorset Spitfire Fund making the sum of 14s., and a stall for Red Cross funds made 11s. 6d. There is a report of knitting 122 garments for the services, and a 'Social' was held to raise funds for prisoner of war parcels. The WI made a lot of jam using a special sugar ration given to all WIs for this purpose. A secretary for jam making was appointed. The jam had to be made to specified recipes and sold at a fixed price. The schoolchildren picked large quantities of blackberries for this.

In December 1939 Piddlehinton WI celebrated its twenty-first birthday with a Christmas party in the schoolroom. Miss Way, the president, gave a birthday cake, and Mrs Riggs, who had attended the very first meeting, gave a toast to the Institute. All members brought presents they had made costing less than one shilling, and drew lots for which present they would receive.

In 1944 a flower show was held at the Rectory with 120 entries. In 1968 the WI celebrated their Golden Jubilee with a Christmas party. After the turkey supper, the celebration cake was cut by Mrs Churchill, their oldest member.

Sadly, in 1969 it was decided to close down because of the lack of members. It was hoped those who remained would join Piddletrenthide. In 1979 the Piddletrenthide WI became the Piddle Valley WI incorporating Piddlehinton.

△   The WI's twenty-first birthday. In the picture are Mrs Gundry, Mrs Vincent, Mrs Gerrard, Mrs T. Reid, Mrs Vera Vincent, Mrs J. Gregory, Mrs Head, Miss Park, Miss Margaret Vincent, Mrs Bob Gregory, Mrs Chute, Miss Way, Mrs Riggs, Mrs Smith, Mrs Walford, Mrs Smith, Mrs Bagg, Mrs Fellowes and Mrs Croft

△   Mrs Churchill cutting the cake at the Golden Jubilee party. Some of the people in the picture are Mrs Davison, Mrs Smeeth, Mrs Stacey, Jill Diggins, Mrs Parsley, Mrs Rose, Mrs Gerrard, Angela Martin, Ann Reed (née Dyke), Mrs Tory, Mrs Diggins and Doreen Sawyer

▷
The Brownie pack in 1946. They are Naomi Baker, Margaret Abbott, Dorothy Waldon, Miss Haydon, Phyllis Sturmey, Christine Davis, Doris Waldon, Pauline Mendleson, Judith Baker, Jean Harvey and Phyllis Abbott

SINGING COMPETITION.—The Puddlehinton Cub pack were very successful at the district singing competition for Cubs at the W.I. Hall, Dorchester, on Saturday. The Cubmistress, Miss Mayo, entered only four Cubs, but they finished with the highest marks of 86 per cent. The Pack was commended on its fine rendering of that favourite old camp song, "Poor Old Michael Finnigan!" The Cubs were trained by Miss Way, of Puddlehinton, and she is to be congratulated on the success of the Cubs in finishing ahead of packs from towns and much larger villages.

△
Report of the Cubs' singing competition in 1938

△
The bellringers' outing in 1950. They are Ben Cheeseman, Paul Field, Fred Davis, Dorothy Warden, Ruth Jeanes, Christine Davis and Doris Warden

In the past there have been **Cubs, Brownies** and **Guides** in the village and there is still a Brownie pack today. A Cub pack was started in the village in the 1920s by Mrs Belgrave. The Cubs met at West Lodge. When Mrs Belgrave became ill, Miss Mayo took charge of the pack. In 1938, although there were only five members, the pack entered and won the Dorset Singing Competition in Dorchester. Many of their rival packs were thirteen or fourteen in number.

It seems that **Scouts** from Piddlehinton joined the Piddletrenthide group. The boys could often be seen packed into Mrs Chute's car, some standing on the running board, being taken to their weekly meetings (Mrs Chute was the rector's wife). Guides met at West Lodge for a short period, later they joined the Piddletrenthide group. A Brownie pack was formed by Miss Susan Churchill early in the war and met in the old Reading Room. After Susan Churchill's marriage, Miss Haydon, the village schoolteacher, ran the pack. They then met at the Rectory. There is still a flourishing pack today run by Mrs Naomi Smeeth (née Baker), seen in the 1946 Brownie group.

There were the usual church groups: the **Choir**, the **Mothers' Union**, the **Sunday School** (run by the rectors' wives on Sunday afternoons) and the **Bellringers**. There were annual outings for all these groups in most years.

Every year there is a church fête in aid of funds. They were always held at the Rectory, and this continued when the church sold the Rectory to Mr and Mrs Rex Lovelace. When Rex Lovelace became ill, the current pattern of alternating with West Lodge began. A marquee was used in which to serve teas, until the cost for its hire outstripped the takings on teas. Now we have to chance the weather. Piddlehinton used to have tug–of–war competitions against Piddletrenthide across the river, at the fête. There has always been a fancy dress competition but in recent years only children have taken part. There are many stalls and side shows and it is always an enjoyable day with good profits.

In 1939, '30 aspirants' are recorded by the rector as 'attending a weekly dancing class for chaps'. Also in 1939 there was a **Men's Club** with forty members. They hired the school for their meetings where they played darts, bagatelle, shove ha'penny, draughts and cards. There was a very successful theatrical group, **'The Bright Sparks'**, in the 1930s and 1940s. They entertained the village and many others with singing, recitations (often in Dorset dialect) and short plays. They were very popular and much in demand. Among their members, Wyn Gerrard, Vera Vincent and Betty Joyce all remember what a lot of fun they had.

In the 1940s there was a very strong **Youth Club** run by Miss Rose Way. Dances and whist drives were held most weeks in the school or the Reading Room, but profits in those days were small. The Youth Club once represented Dorset at a Folk Dance Festival at the Albert Hall. For most of them it was their first visit to London. Shortly after the war they often played table tennis with the 'Displaced Persons', who mostly came from Latvia and Lithuania, at their camp on top of Cerne Hill.

Records also show that there was a **Slate Club** and even an **Octogenarians Group** who met at the New Inn every week back in the 1930s.

◁
George Damen and family with their horse and cart decorated for the fête

▷
Mrs Riggs in the 1920s with her bicycle decorated for the fête

Pyddle Hinton Parish Magazine

AUGUST, 1897.

The Queen's Diamond Jubilee was spent here very pleasantly. As the Rector was in London, no service was held on the Tuesday, but on Sunday a Special Thanksgiving was offered, for the many blessings vouchsafed to the nation during the sixty years' reign of our beloved Sovereign. All the parishioners had liberally contributed towards a public dinner for the adults, and tea for the children, who also had Jubilee Mugs given them, and the meals were enlivened by selections played by the Weymouth Band, which had been engaged for the day. During the afternoon and evening there were sports and dancing, and owing to the careful supervision of the Committee, everything passed off well, and the day was a great success. Our thanks are due to Mr J. Riggs for kindly lending his barn and field, and to all those who generously gave their time and thoughts towards making others happy. Long live our gracious Queen!

Pyddle Hinton Parish Magazine.

JULY, 1899.

On Thursday, June 9th, the Choir, together with some members of the Women's Union, had a most enjoyable trip to Weymouth. Everyone having assembled at the Rectory, after prayers the party started for the station, some in a brake, some on bicycles, and the remainder in the Rector's pony carriage. By the courtesy of the Stationmaster and Mr. Reed, the Superintendent, who always takes a kindly interest in outings from Pyddle Hinton, comfortable seats were speedily obtained, and shortly after Weymouth was reached. The party then dispersed, to amuse themselves as they liked, meeting again at one o'clock and at five for dinner and tea, which, as before, was well provided for at Lumley's. We hope all those who took part in the excursion had a happy and profitable day. We were extremely sorry that one of those who had been looking forward to coming at the last moment found herself unable. We need not say that she was much missed. As several people, when it was too late to arrange for them, wished they could be of the party, it has been proposed to start a weekly holiday fund, and Mrs. Hawksley will, from this date, be glad to receive not less than 2d. a week, and as much more as people like, so that next summer any one who likes can go. Should they pay more than the trip will cost, the overplus will be returned, and if from untoward circumstances people are unable to keep up their weekly payments, their money will be given back.

It is hoped that in the course of next month the Band of Hope will have a Tea in the Rectory field.

The Old Fashioned Wedding group. They are Fred Hawkins, Arthur Jeanes, Tom Cosh, Florrie Jeanes, Jim Jeanes, George Hansford, Mrs Murphy, Mrs Reid, Molly Jeanes, Margaret Jeanes, Grace Ford, Mrs Hawkins, Mrs Gregory, Frank Jeanes (Bridegroom), Annie Jeanes (Bride), Mrs Ellen Gregory, Miss Neal and Alf Dyke
▽

Celebrations

Piddlehinton people love to celebrate. Over the years they have celebrated jubilees, coronations, royal weddings and war victories, with wonderful tea parties, sports, firework displays and dancing. The various organizations have gone on outings to the seaside or to shows – every year there have been Christmas parties to look forward to.

In 1934, to celebrate the centenary of the Tolpuddle Martyrs, an Old Fashioned Wedding was staged in the Rectory garden.

◁
Charabanc outing to Weymouth in 1920. On board are Florrie Jeanes, Mrs Bagg, Mrs Saint, Mrs C. Gregory, Mrs Bob Gregory and Mrs Riggs

▷
Sunday school outing to Weymouth in 1927. They are Bert Saint, Mabel Saint, Jack Gerrard, Mabel Gerrard, Florrie Jeanes, Bill Jeanes, Ted Jeanes and Wilf Saint

Shroving

On Shrove Tuesday it used to be the custom that the village children would go shroving, calling at houses in the village and singing;

> Here we come a-shroving
> For a piece of pancake
> Or a piece of truckle cheese
> Of your own making.
> Hot pot the pans hot
> The cupboard door is open
> Pray Missus, good Missus,
> If your heart be open
> Here we come without our bags
> Afraid we won't get nothing.

They were usually given a few sweets, an apple, a piece of cheese, or a few coppers tossed on the grass. They all scrambled for the coppers and the strongest got the most. Miss Drake, at her shop in the High Street, would throw a few sweets out of the door.

Chapter 9

THE TWO WORLD WARS

PUDDLEHINTON.

THE APPEAL FOR RECRUITS.—A successful recruiting meeting was held in the Schoolroom on Tuesday, the 1st, when Captain Astell presided, and among those present were Colonel Law and Colonel Gretton, Major and Mrs. Smith, Colonel and Mrs. Saunders, the Rector and Mrs. Newman, Hon. Mrs. Law, Mr. J.E.M. Bridge, Rev. H.A. Folkard, Rev. —, Morland, Messrs. Riggs, Colour-Sergt. Brown, and Miss Riggs. The room was crowded, and the audience very enthusiastic. The Chairman, opening the meeting, referred to the gallant deeds of Dorset men in the past, and particularly of Captain Hardy, and asked "Are we going to be unworthy descendants of the men who fought with him?" He referred to the danger the country was in, and to the cruel treatment of old men, women, and children by the Germans, and said they must all ask themselves the question, "What can I do for my country in this the hour of her need?" and, having found the answer, do it at once. (Loud applause.) Colonel Law outlined the duty of the Territorial Force Association in helping the work of recruiting, and pointed out that everybody could assist in the work. Having touched on the origin of the war and the strategical positions of the European nations, he called upon everybody to help to raise the necessary army required by Lord Kitchener to crush the enemy. He explained the conditions of service now offered to recruits and the number of men that would eventually be required. He said Dorset men always "turned up trumps," but many more recruits from this district were wanted. He concluded by referring to the evil effects of intoxicants on men who were in training, and also warned everybody to obey sentries without question when challenged. (Applause.) Colonel Gretton, who followed, referred to the work of the National Reserve, and the gallant way in which the men had flocked back to the ranks. He asked all the women to try and get their husbands and sweethearts or brothers to join at once and commence their training. He had been surprised to see a large number of young men refrain from joining when so many middle-aged men had done so. All his relatives were in the army, nearly all of them at the front, and he himself hoped to cross the Channel before the war was over to strike a blow for his country. He asked the women to help the work of recruiting, and concluded with a call to the men to "roll up." General Beckett proposed a vote of thanks to the speakers, which was seconded by Major Smith, and the National Anthem concluded the meeting.

△
Shortly after the start of the First World War, a recruiting meeting was held in the village school. This excerpt from the *Dorset County Chronicle* of 10 September 1914 describes the meeting

The 1914–18 War

Fifty-six men from Piddlehinton served in the forces in the 1914–18 war. Seventeen of them were killed – approximately one in three of the able-bodied men in the village.

The War Memorial

After the 1914–18 war, a committee was set up in the village to decide in what way Piddlehinton should commemorate these men. The secretary of the committee was Col. Belgrave. The options considered included: a Memorial Hall, a water supply for the village, a hand bier, the church bells to be made to ring, a window pane in the

△
Walter Gale, Private in the Grenadiers, who was killed at Gallipoli in 1917, aged 20

◁
Pioneer R. J. (Jack) Groves of the
Royal Engineers. He transferred
from the Dorset Regiment during
the war

▷
Corporal Arthur Gale and Private
Thomas Gale, who both served in
the Canadian Army. They had
both emigrated to Canada before
the war, but were born in
Piddlehinton

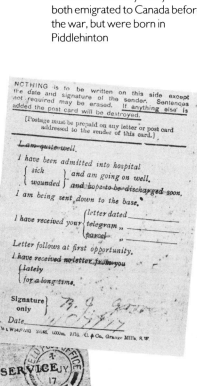

▷
The official card that Jack Groves
was allowed to send, telling his
family he had been wounded. He
was badly burned, especially his
hands

△
Private Tommy Cosh of the
Dorset Regiment

△
Frank Samways in Piddlehinton some years after the war. He lost his arm when a stray shell exploded near him when he was playing pitch-ha'penny behind the lines

church to be dedicated to each man who fell. The decision was to build the Memorial Cross that stands at the centre of the village today.

The following men from Piddlehinton were killed in the First World War: Cecil Dacombe (Dorset Regt), Walter Gale (Dorset Yeomanry), William Collins (Dorset Regt), Ernest Rowe (Dorset Regt), Joseph Bush (Dorset Regt), Frank Gillingham (Dorset Regt), James Levi Dyke (Dorset Regt), James Samways (Dorset Regt), Albert Hardy (Grenadier Guards), Godfrey Astell (North Staffordshire Regt), Frank Rowe ('Canadians'), William Park (Dorset Regt), Walter Jeanes (Grenadier Guards), Frederick Smith (Royal Field Artillery), Edward Robbins (Dorset Regt), Henry Damen (Dorset Regt) and Frank Kent (Dorset Regt).

The sum raised exceeded the cost of the Memorial by £19. 15s. 1d. This was set aside to start a Village Hall Fund. In 1937, to mark the Silver Jubilee of King George V and Queen Mary, the Memorial was railed off with oak posts and chains, and given a substantial concrete base.

▷
The War Memorial was dedicated at a special ceremony in 1921. It was made by Hounsell's Stone and Granite Works of Broadway, Weymouth, who made crosses for many Dorset villages. It cost £146.4s.0d. including £10 for hiring a horse to pull the base. The masons are shown here erecting the memorial

Armistice Day Dinners

For many years after the war an Armistice Day dinner, for all those who had served in the forces during the war, was held at West Lodge at the invitation of Col. Belgrave. A long table was set up in the old studio on the first floor. Cdr Churchill and Col. Belgrave sat one at each end, each carving a joint. The meal always ended with apple dumplings, and there was a barrel of beer downstairs. Stories were told and songs were sung. The last verse of a song which was sung every year ran:

> and some did not come home again
> we think of them today.
> The men of Piddlehinton
> and the Piddlehinton men.

Men who had left the village were always invited back for the occasion.

The 1939–45 War

Fortunately, only four men from Piddlehinton were killed in the Second World War. Their names were added to the War Memorial; Roland Bennet (RAF), Henry Cross (Royal Artillery), Albert Dyke (RASC) and Walter Welsh (RAF/VR).

◁
Captain Robert Belgrave, Royal Horse Artillery, with his tank crew on the German frontier

The Home Guard

Renamed the Home Guard by Churchill, the Local Defence Volunteers were formed in 1940, to face enemy invasion. Their job was to deliver Churchill's promise, 'We shall fight them on the beaches . . . we shall fight them in the fields and in the streets.' This they fully expected to do, although armed only with shotguns, pitchforks and 'Molotov cocktails'.

The Dorset Home Guard was commanded by Gen. Sir Henry

This Home Guard company includes the Piddlehinton Platoon, among them Herbie Downton, Jack Way, Wilf Saint, Len Black, Edgar Tory, Reg Cosh, Tommy Cosh, Charlie Jeanes, Philip Tory, John Chapman, Mr Jackson, Mr Phillips and Bill Gregory

Jackson of Piddletrenthide, with Col. John Belgrave of Piddlehinton as his Chief of Staff. Piddlehinton, commanded by Major John Chapman of Higher Waterston, was grouped with Bockhampton, with the idea of holding the line of the River Frome against enemy troops landing at Weymouth. Such an event would have been signalled by the ringing of the church bells, which were otherwise silent throughout the war.

As the threat of invasion receded, the Home Guard, better equipped and trained (all in their spare time and without pay), gradually took over more conventional, and often boring jobs in order to free the army for the invasion of France. But perhaps the Piddlehinton Platoon's finest hour was the capture near Doles Wood of the pilot of a German plane, shot down during the Battle of Britain. Landing by parachute and considerably shaken, he must have been still more shaken to see the huntsman of the South Dorset Hunt, bearing down on him at full gallop with a Home Guardsman's rifle in his hand and his hounds around him.

Piddlehinton's Wartime Instructions

The following are some of the wartime instructions written by the rector. Some were put on the village notice-board, others were circulated to parishioners.

AIR RAID PRECAUTIONS
Warden: The rector
In charge of First Aid party: Mrs Chute
HQ: The Rectory

FIRE PARTY
Mr Cyril Green in charge
Captain Fellowes' stable the HQ; Hose there
3 Stirrup pumps: One in Mrs Lovelace's garage
                  One in Captain Fellowes' open garage
                  One in Rectory stable
    All available for anyone to use without first asking the Fire Party.
    Signal: Ringing of the Dinner Bell to be hung beside the forge for public use.
    In case of enemy attack, wait till the first phase of danger is over. It seems unreasonable to go into the roads when machine guns are firing and there are bombs dropping.

GAS
Please make sure that everyone has a mask which fits and is in good condition. The signal for gas is given by a rattle. When the danger is over, a bell will be rung.

WAR SAVINGS CERTIFICATES
Remember that if you can spare any money now for saving, you may be glad of it later on, and the Government would like to borrow it through the system of certificates. Stamps can be bought towards buying one.

AIR RAIDS
It is very tempting to stand outside watching an air battle; but I would remind you that bullets fired in the air must come to earth somewhere and it is most unwise to stand outside, or near glass windows, when enemy action is taking place directly above the village.

HOME GUARD OR LDV
Rex Lovelace is in charge of our section. They are summoned to their HQ at Manor Farm by ringing of the church bells or violent tooting of a motor horn.
    If there should be fighting here, civilians should stay indoors or in their private dug-outs.

SALVAGE

There are dumps for scrap iron in Lackington, Piddlehinton and Muston.

Aluminium can be brought to the Rectory. Paper and cardboard is collected weekly by Miss Mayo.

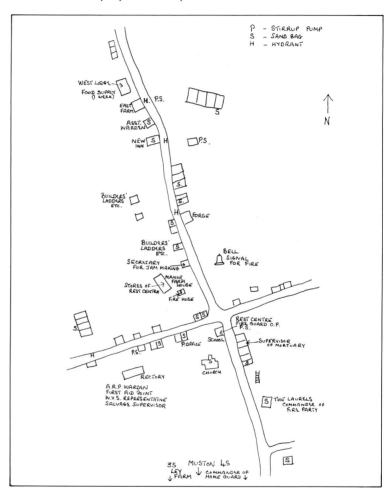

▷
The village defences according to a map drawn by the rector, Rev. Chute

The Mysterious Parachute Mine

The *Dorset Constabulary* reported the landing of a mysterious parachute mine near Doles Wood in 1941. It was a delayed-action enemy weapon containing many booby traps, deliberately aimed at killing the members of HMS *Vernon's* skilled anti-mine establishment at Portsmouth. Guided to the huge object by Constable Fish, some of these courageous experts came to Piddlehinton and spent nearly a week cutting into the mine, step by step, rendering booby trap after booby trap harmless as they went.

Perambulator Service

When several mothers with their small children came to Piddlehinton as evacuees, the rector started holding perambulator services on Friday afternoons, particularly intended for mothers with very young children. They lasted about half an hour and anyone was welcome. 'If everyone in the church has a baby' the rector wrote, 'they will all be sympathetic and no one can mind if your child does fidget a bit and cry. If there is too much screaming, we'll sing a hymn and see if we can drown it out.'

Piddlehinton Camp

The land to build Piddlehinton Army Camp was requisitioned by the War Department in 1937. The land was compulsorily purchased for £31 an acre, from Philip Tory, who was growing corn on it. The land was supposed to be returned to agricultural use after the emergency but this did not happen. The camp made a huge impact on the village.

When the camp was built, a lot of men who helped build it had lodgings in the village. Men from the village also helped. They would often bring their wives or girlfriends to the village, and villagers would put them up for weekends. Some still come to visit today. Church parades were held every Sunday morning when the whole of Rectory Road was full of parading soldiers.

Many soldiers have passed through the camp. The 1st Division Americans, Red Berets (Parachute Regt), Royal Engineers, Pay Corps, Hussars, King's Dragoon Guards, Royal Artillery, Royal Welch Fusiliers and many more. The Fusiliers were often seen taking their mascot goat for a walk through the village.

The American soldiers invited all the local schoolchildren to a Christmas party in 1943, collecting them in large lorries. A wonderful time was had by all. The food was delicious, one delicacy

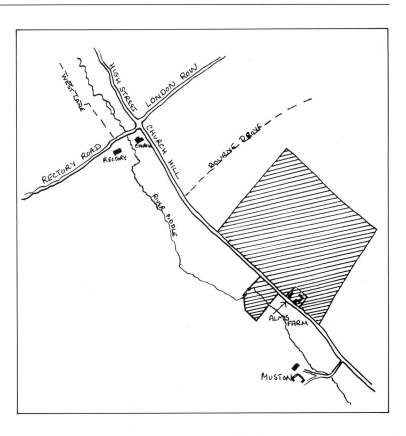

▷
The land requisitioned for
Piddlehinton Camp in 1937

being peach and ham sandwiches. The Americans were very
generous towards the village children, giving them sweets and
chewing gum when they met in the street – often throwing these
treats from their lorries. In 1943, rides on a Bren Gun Carrier were
one of the attractions at the village fête. There were often dances and
parties at the camp to which locals were invited. Several 'war babies'
were left behind; some soldiers were married in Piddlehinton
church.

One famous soldier stationed at the camp was Rex Whistler, the
painter. During his stay he painted a mural on the wall of one of the
huts. Unfortunately he was killed in action, and his painting
obliterated by redecoration at a later date. Famous people came to
entertain the troops, including Glenn Miller and his band, and Joe
Louis the boxer.

During the war the village was overrun with soldiers and the camp
appeared to be bursting at the seams. The roads around the village
cross had to be built up with concrete to stand the weight of the
tanks.

When the D–Day invasion was about to begin, convoys lasting all
day and all night passed through the village. There were a lot of air
raids over the village as the camp was a target for the Germans.

Several landmines were dropped nearby; fortunately they did not explode. A searchlight battery was set up on the Bourne road (near where the grass drier is today), to protect the camp. Although food was very short, no one in Piddlehinton went hungry. Most people had a few hens in their back gardens, and there was always a rabbit, and in the spring, rook pie and lambs' tails. People also grew a lot of vegetables.

The camp operated for a long time after the war, and summer camps went on using the field near Fishers Lane. Leslie Thomas, the author, has happy memories of two weeks' 'reserve training' at the camp in the summer of 1951. For a short time in 1972, Ugandan Asians stayed at the camp, their children attending the village school.

◁
The Prince's Trust used the camp in 1984. It caused great excitement when Prince Charles visited, and local people were able to meet him. Here he is seen chatting to villagers at the camp

THE DUMMY CAMP

A dummy military post was built up Lackington Drove to lure attacks away from Piddlehinton Camp. It included one or two Nissen huts. A few parachute mines landed near it and children from the village raced to the site to collect pieces of the parachute silk.

Some of Geoff Lord's Memories as an Evacuee in Piddlehinton

It seems as though it was only yesterday that I was evacuated to Piddlehinton with my mother and my brother, Ron. The day of my arrival to the village has always remained firmly fixed in my memory. The date was 8 March 1941, and I was fortunate in being billeted with Col. Belgrave and his sister, Miss Sybil, who lived at West Lodge.

Ron and Geoff Lord, evacuees to Piddlehinton

I was about seven years old when the Second World War broke out, and before coming to Piddlehinton, I had already been evacuated on four previous occasions. My penultimate move was with Miss Sybil Belgrave's cousins at Eastbourne, and it was through this connection that it was my good fortune to be evacuated to the Piddle Valley.

Because of the vast overcrowding of schools at the various places to which I was evacuated, it was not possible to commence my education again until I came to Piddlehinton. At the beginning of the war every person in the country was issued with a gas mask, and if you forgot to take it with you to school, home again you had to go to fetch it! After staying at West Lodge for about 12 months, my parents were offered the tenancy of one of the cottages at West Lodge, and there I lived until I was married. After coming from a home with all modern conveniences, I found it rather difficult to accept living in a cottage with only one cold water tap, one electric light in the living room and no waterborne sanitation. My mother must have found it rather difficult cooking with paraffin after using gas for so many years.

Living in London I never had the pleasure of seeing cows, sheep, pigs, birds and wild animals. This was a completely new way of life for me, and what an immense pleasure it has all been. We were immediately made to feel very welcome by everyone in Piddlehinton, and we soon adapted and took part in the country ways and life of the village. Some of the locals used to affectionately refer to me as 'Thik Refugee', but I knew differently, I was 'Thik Evacuee'.

As children we had our part to play in the war, picking blackberries for jam, and rose hips which were processed into syrup. For two weeks each September we went potato picking.

Birthdays and Christmas were almost like any other days during the war years. Food and sweets were very scarce, so it was not always possible to have any real treats. Toys were also scarce. Our Christmas lunch always consisted of two baked rabbits, stuffed with thyme and parsley. Chickens were an unknown luxury.

A great feeling of 'esprit de corps' prevailed during the war. Everyone did all they could to help one another, and this played an important part in helping our country to achieve victory.

I was very pleased that my parents decided to stay in Piddlehinton after the war was over. I married a local girl, Fay Jeanes, in September 1953, and have continued to make Piddlehinton my home.

Chapter 10

A PICTORIAL RAMBLE
THROUGH THE VILLAGE

At the beginning of the twentieth century, most of the cottages, outbuildings and walls in Piddlehinton were still thatched. Although several remain, a number have since disappeared for various reasons. Three major fires destroyed much of the High Street.

Amy Neades of White Lackington can recall the Piddletrenthide fire engine being pushed down the road to fight the 1925 blaze, but all in vain. In 1927, a brick house was built on the site of the old millhouse by Watts, the builders. The roadside house was never replaced.

In December 1932, when Mr and Mrs Gregory were living in the High Street (the present number 7), Emily gave birth to her first son, John. The following day the house caught fire, and Mrs Gregory had

Piddlehinton village centre from Rectory Road approach
▽

◁

In 1925 traction engine sparks set fire to this roadside home of Mr and Mrs Jack Groves, daughter Nora and son Les. Jack Groves was out cycling on his daily rounds as postman when the fire began. In later life he became a farmhand for Rex Lovelace

▷

In 1925 fire spread to the adjacent millhouse called 'Waterfall'. Annie Smith is seen outside this house in 1887. Fred and Amelia Smith lived there at the time of the fire. Mrs Smith died shortly afterwards – 16 June – owing to ill-health, old age, and from the shock of the fire

▷
This row of cottages (seen in 1905) further along the High Street (opposite the New Inn) was burnt in two fires

to be carried to another bedroom whilst the fire brigade put the fire out. This house now has a slate roof!

A year later, in December 1933, the 'Great Fire' of Piddlehinton left three families homeless. Apparently, Mr Stacey, who lived in one of the cottages, had used a paraffin rag to light his fire that morning. It caught alight a smouldering beam in the chimney. Neighbours joined the Dorchester Fire Brigade in a 9-hour struggle against the fire, hindered by a water shortage and high winds. Robert Belgrave (who took some photographs with a Box Brownie) remembers the fire engine arriving from Piddletrenthide drawn by

△ The Great Fire of 1933 in the High Street △

△
At one time, fire brigades were private organizations. Insurance had to be taken out if the owner of the building wished any fire to be fought by firemen. A plaque would then be displayed to signify that payment was assured. Inglenook Cottage in Rectory Road (formerly Paynes Cottage), a Dorset longhouse, has survived several centuries and bears this plaque ▷

△
Mr and Mrs Gundry and their son Alan lived in this house in the High Street before it burnt down

cart-horses, with men running beside. However, when the fire engine's hoses were connected to the mill stream, the hand pump was not strong enough for the water to reach the roof, and buckets had to be used instead. One of the cottages was occupied by a retired butler of Lord Wynford, called Mr Smart. He had received some watches for long service, which he kept in a cabinet upstairs. Mr Head, from White's Dairy, tried to help him get the cabinet downstairs when the fire started. However, the roof fell in and they had to abandon the cabinet and make their escape. The watches were never found. Only the people in the house on the end saved any belongings. The date of the fire was John Gregory's first birthday!

Several thatched cottages and barns remain in the village, although some are disguised by late twentieth century renovation.

△
Mrs Dyke's cottage, in London Row, just above Piddlehinton Cross, fell down in the 1950s

△
Many buildings and outbuildings fell into disrepair – often owing to poor upkeep by the landlord. They were later abandoned and bulldozed. The Riggs family lived in one such cottage close to the New Inn, behind the white railings. Other buildings alongside and opposite the inn, suffered a similar fate

△
Miss Margaret Jeanes in 1930, in the garden of the millhouse. The thatched outbuildings of the forge are behind, on the opposite side of the road

▷
The 'New' Pound looking down Church Hill. It was bulldozed in 1975

△
The walls and outbuildings of the Manor were thatched until recent years

△
Glebe Cottage has been named both Glebe Farmhouse and Rectory Cottage in the past. The former farmhouse for the Glebe lands dates from the seventeenth century. A dairy was attached to the side of the house when cows were kept on the Glebe holding. Dairy farmers included William John Symes (1903) and George Damen (1920)

△
Charlie Jeanes, gardener to the rector for 32 years from 1932 onwards, and his wife Evelyn (née Smith) lived at Rectory Cottage. The Rectory and cottage were sold together in 1964

▷
The Laurels (now The Beeches)

The Laurels, a large thatched house to the south of the village centre, had stables and a groom's cottage next door. The house has a mysterious past. A nun is said to have been murdered in the attic bedroom (top window). Mr Charles Mayo held the copyhold from Eton College in the late nineteenth century until his early death. A succession of tenants, including Albert Lane, William Mayo, James Rowe, E. Westmacott, Mrs Hendley and the Money family, all followed whilst the Mayo family still held the copyhold for the life of the 'two Churchills'. On the death of Philip Churchill (1 January 1930), Mr H. G. Mayo tried to buy The Laurels from Eton. However, it was sold in 1936 to the sitting tenant, Cyril Green. During the time in which Cyril Green and his family lived there (until the early 1960s), they were very happy, despite the 'presence' – a rush of air which passes from the attic rooms, through a door, and down the back stairs to the servants' quarters. One land girl refused to stay in the back attic room as 'something walks there'. Another land girl stayed in the front attic room aware of it, but unafraid. The house has been renamed The Beeches.

The Royal Historic Monuments survey lists White's Dairy House as East Farmhouse, the same name as the neighbouring slated house which is of a later period. Perhaps it was originally so, as it bears a 1622 datestone near the eaves on the north side, and medieval cusped tracery near a window. The banded flint and rubble walls, with occasional bands of ashlar, show a striking join where a seventeenth-century extension was added, followed by a further extension in the eighteenth century. Outbuildings, with a large thatched barn alongside (all of the same period), formed a large unit

△
Further south, outside the village centre is an isolated thatched former farmhouse called Little Piddle Farmhouse (photograph taken 23 April 1923). It is possibly a Dorset longhouse and would have been a central feature of the Manor of Little Piddle. It was later renamed Lawrence Mead

△
Another large and old thatched house stands to the north of the village – White's Dairy House

△
A row of four houses in London Row used as poorhouses in earlier times. The walls are made of rubble. All four were reputedly sold in the 1940s for a total of £100. They still stand as two enlarged cottages

◁
Mabel Saint, wife of the Piddlehinton carpenter and funeral director Bert Saint, outside their High Street home, formerly called Davis Farmhouse. It has been renovated in recent years and renamed Longpuddle

◁

Lantern Cottage in the days when it was the village Post Office (before the present Post Office was built). A water pump replaced the old well on the Green. Lantern Cottage has been converted to a private dwelling. The cottage next door also survives

△

Mary Hardy, during her time as schoolmistress in the village, painted two ash trees on the Green in 1876. Was this artistic licence or perhaps a true record of a second tree which may have stood before the War Memorial?

◁

The thatched farm cottages which still stand on the junction of Rectory Road and High Street. The old ash tree with the War Memorial dominated the village green

used as the dairy of the Piddlehinton Manor. More centrally, several cottages have been preserved.

Piddlehinton Cross, at the junction of London Road, Rectory Road, Church Hill and High Street, has always provided a natural focus for the village. The Green is a small grassed triangular mound at the crossroads. It bears the War Memorial, a bench seat, an old water pump (once a well), and an ash tree. A younger ash tree was planted in Silver Jubilee year, to one side of the mound, as a replacement for the previous ancient and diseased ash tree. The old tree had a hollow trunk (since before the erection of the War Memorial!) and was finally removed after much surgery, in 1987.

Slate has replaced thatch in other noteworthy buildings. Bridge House, in the centre of the village, is rumoured to have been Piddlehinton Manor Farmhouse at an early date. During conversion in 1985, builders found pieces of church masonry in the walls, and

△

The Green in the days when the well was used by surrounding cottages

▷
Bridge House was refronted in
1866 and bears a panel, 'C.M.
1866'. It has recently been
restored and extended

△
The bridge bears the date 1834
inscribed on the north parapet. It
has a single round arch of ashlar. A
plaque, attached sideways (during
later reconstruction?), is inscribed,
'NOTICE TO OWNERS AND
DRIVERS OF TRACTION
ENGINES. THIS BRIDGE IS
INSUFFICIENT TO CARRY
WEIGHTS BEYOND THE
ORDINARY TRAFFIC OF THE
DISTRICT'

other original fifteenth-century features. These included a stone
fireplace with holes either side of the main lintel. Apparently at the
time of the Wars of the Roses, white or red rose emblems would have
been removed from these holes.

Nearby, in Rectory Road, the main bridge over the River Piddle,
is a central feature of the village. A disused ford remains on the
northern side. Perhaps this is on the site of the bridge referred to in
the overseers accounts, '1745 August 23 paide thomas day for
mending the bucket bridge 5–0'; '1746 February 5 paide Robert
brodbey for waling the bucket bridge 8d'.

Manor House, alongside, was the Manor Farmhouse for many
years. It was rebuilt in 1866 by George Mayo. The original structure
was a very old building covered with thatch. It was destroyed by
fire, probably just prior to being rebuilt. The only rooms which
remain unaltered from 1866 are a washroom (with a copper cauldron

▷
The Manor Farmhouse and stable
block

fed from a well in the kitchen), and a sewing room upstairs. A large inglenook fireplace with a bread oven also remains. The stable block alongside was rebuilt in brick, flint and slate in 1867. The ground floor comprised a carriage house leading to the old tack room. Above the carriage house, an external staircase led to the old village Reading Room. This was used by the local community as a meeting place. Reading Rooms were built in this area at that time, as Victorian society had become concerned about the increased drinking in public houses. It has recently been converted to a dwelling. Other outbuildings include storerooms, an old game larder, a garden room and a loose-box.

The 1861 census records landowning farmer George Mayo, a widower, living in the house with his three sons and a daughter, a governess, two house servants, and a laundress. By 1871, only one son and the daughter were still at home, with a housekeeper, cook and a housemaid. Other occupants (usually farmers) in later years included, Joseph Roper (1875), Joseph Riggs (1890), later Levi Riggs then Miss Riggs, V. de Meric (1927), H. Smart (1931), Captain T. Fellowes (1939, throughout and after the war). Captain Fellowes was the last farmer of the manorial land to live there. After his time, a succession of tenants lived in the house until Eton sold it, in 1964, to Thomas Bryan.

Back in the centre of the village, across the road from the churchyard and school, is a row of farm cottages with slate roofs which were most probably thatched at one time. They are known as Church Hill Cottages.

Along the High Street, Ivy Cottage, next to the Manor, was once the home of the village policeman. Next to the blacksmith's cottage, opposite the forge, is another slate-roofed house where a boot-repairer lived. Further along the High Street, a house, opposite the New Inn, was built for Mr and Mrs Smart as a replacement for their thatched cottage which burnt down in 1933. The garden has been used in recent years as a commercial nursery. A row of four cottages, called Coronation Cottages (built for Eton at the time of George VI's coronation), was constructed next to the Smarts' house.

On the left, next to East Farm House, stands West Lodge. Originally a square flint and stone house, it was built by Stephen Iles,

This early postcard shows Church Hill Cottages. Two walls no longer exist – one around the cottage garden, the other at the end of the school

East Farm House, just beyond White's Dairy House, was the residence of the Lovelace family for generations. Several Lovelaces acted as rent collectors for Eton College. The 'Nag Stable and Gig House' opposite is now converted as a dwelling named the Old Stables

In 1812 Rev. Churchill foreclosed and sold the house to John Baverstock Knight. He also bought 'a workshop and a room with chambers over' standing near the house and built a large first-floor studio connecting them, with kitchen and domestic offices below, most of which now constitute South West Lodge

△
Col. and Mrs Belgrave's trap outside the coach house at West Lodge c. 1920

of Godmanstone, in 1779. He and his new bride, Jane, moved in from their cottage next door shortly after their wedding. He must have over-extended himself building the house as he took a mortgage from the Rev. Churchill of Muston. There is a memorial to Jane Iles in the church.

The Rev. Churchill foreclosed on the mortgage in 1812 and the house was sold to John Baverstock Knight. As the fee for his services as Commissioner for the Piddlehinton Enclosure Act in 1835, he acquired some small fields west of the house. He planted a line of trees on the down at the western limit of his new property, most of which still stand. The house was sold to Major and Mrs Astell in 1862. They sold it to Col. and Mrs Belgrave in 1917 whose family still live there.

This completes the ramble! The church, Rectory and school are mentioned at length elsewhere, and all contribute to the traditional character of the village. The heart of the village remains picturesque, despite the ravages of fires, bulldozers, and the changes in rural life.

▷
The Astells 'modernized' these cottages in 1898 by raising the roof and putting tiles over the thatch. A single skin of bricks with small paned windows was put on the front elevation only, in front of the cob wall, to give the cottages a Victorian appearance

△
In 1759 Stephen Iles built himself a cob and thatch cottage on a piece of land at the north end of the village called Romaynes tenement. His initials and the date are carved in the roof timbers

▷
In 1975, West Lodge Cottages were renovated and amalgamated into one called Romaynes Cottage. The tiled roof was redone and the thatch removed from under it, as this photo shows

Chapter 11

EVENTS AND LEGENDS
IN PIDDLEHINTON

The Arrival of Electricity and the Telephone in the Village

In 1934, the Trades Union Council celebrated the centenary of the deportation of the Tolpuddle Martyrs, by erecting a row of Memorial Cottages at Tolpuddle. These were to have all the modern conveniences of the time, including electricity. As Piddlehinton lay on the route chosen to bring the power cables to Tolpuddle from Bristol, the village also benefited from the centenary by being connected to the National Grid. Until then lighting had been by oil lamps in every village home.

The village was first connected to the telegraph in 1898. In 1948 a telephone kiosk 'has appeared in the village', wrote the rector, the Rev. J. C. Chute. 'No need for people to use the Rectory phone any more!' But the kiosk was not the advantage that was expected. There were many complaints because it was a party line, and villagers often had to wait a considerable time to get through as the line was busy. It stayed on a party line until 1961.

Water Worries and Bad Weather

In the early 1920s there was a great drought, when all the wells dried up and water had to be carted from Morning Well in Piddletrenthide, a source of the River Piddle. It was sold to villagers by Mr Lovelace at 1d. a bucket, and everyone had to take double on Saturdays for the weekend.

There were anxieties over water shortages each year. If it was a dry summer, men had to be lowered down the wells, to dig out deposits and deepen them, all in the hope of improving the water supply. Water was collected by bucket from the mill leat for wash day.

'A Suggested Water Supply', from a newspaper cutting dated January 1935, reports: 'A parish meeting called at the request of the Piddlehinton Women's Institute, was held to consider the provision of a water supply. The Sanitary Inspector was in attendance. After

△

In 1928, a very bad winter brought a great snow drift by Snowdrop Corner and over Waterston ridge, cutting off the village. Men from the village, working as a team, gradually dug a way through. Others enjoyed skating on Gaskins water meadow

discussion, a committee of three, Commander Churchill, Colonel Belgrave and another, was appointed to canvass the village to find out how many people would be prepared to take a water supply. The conditions were that the village should pay a shilling a year rate, and water users pay a charge of 12½ per cent on the rateable value of property rated at £4 and over, and a minimum charge of 10s. per cottage of rateable value £3 or under. Rev. Newman said that one of the pumps was very unsatisfactory and it took seventy strokes to fill a bucket the previous night.'

In many winters there were bad floods in the village. People sometimes had to be taken by horse and cart from the cross to near the Rectory. The report of the gypsy wedding, below, mentions these floods.

Gypsy Wedding at Piddlehinton

As reported in the *Dorset County Chronicle*, 2 February 1937.

FAMOUS GYPSY FAMILIES AT WEDDING

Villagers saw a novel sight on Monday morning when Alice White, beautiful member of a gypsy family famous in the South of England, splashed her way through floods to the parish church for her wedding. The groom, Mr Stephen Button of Lytchett Matravers, cycled the 20 miles from his smallholding, and arrived in time for the service. The bride was dressed in a vivid scarlet and green outfit, and rode to church in a dog cart. The ceremony was attended by many members of the Romany tribe, including such noted families as the Hughes, Benhams and Coopers.

Guest of honour at the camp on the hill at Lackington was Mrs Benham, widow of "Wold Ben", uncrowned gypsy king, whose burial at Dorchester recently attracted so much attention. With her were three sons, including Tom, the 18-year-old acrobat dancer.

The camp, which consisted of six caravans, was dangerously close to the flooded area, and the van wheels were embedded in thick mud. The bride had to pass through more floods on the Puddlehinton–Charminster road before reaching the church. The couple were married by the Rector, the Rev. W. G. Newman, who told a reporter that he was greatly impressed by the conduct and system prevailing at the camp, which he had visited several times during the period spent complying with the residential qualification.

The church entrance was surrounded by crowds of villagers, and to make the occasion more festive, left-over Christmas decorations had been brought from the Post Office, and these were draped around the archway.

A huge cake had been baked and iced by Mr Davies, the local baker. After the service the couple went on ahead of the others, the groom on his bicycle and his bride by his side on foot. The other members of the party left by dog cart. A celebration was held in the evening at the Green Dragon, Puddletrenthide, when many more members of the Romany clan came to wish the couple happiness.

The Witch of Piddlehinton

There have long been stories in Piddlehinton about the village witch. Here is a version which comes from *Dorset Folklore collected in 1897*, by H. Colley March. 'Mr Hardy has made some alterations in the spelling, so that the dialect may be better represented.'

Walter Churchill, coachman to General Astell of West Lodge, 'an honest, honourable, god-fearing man' told this story:

When I was a little chap 'bout eight, I and Jack Wolfral was taking a bit of a walk, and as we comed down drove we seed, both o' us, a hare sot by the stile of the churchyard, where sure, never a hare were seed before nor since; but 'twere this way. We were living to Bourne then, and a neighbour that had the palsy so terr'ble bad he couldn't walk nor guide hisself, and said as he were overlooked, and twold it to a travelling man (a pedlar), and he said if we could say who 'twere as doned it he'd cure 'un. So the poor man said 'twere a woman as lived a long way off. 'Never mind', says the travelling man, 'I'll bring her here in the form o' a hare, and make her cure thee.' So he bid un get a odd number o' folk, and my father were one, to sit up at night and do what he twold un'. And he did say as there were a bottle o' summat hanged up in chimney. And the fire were blinded off, and the travelling man were a-reading verses out of the Bible backward, when just as we was outside the string broke, and the bottle fell, and it broke, and what come o' the hare I can't say. The travelling man was for coming another night to finish the cure, for the man were a sight better already; I seed him myself stand and kick out his leg; but the passen heard o' it and put un off.

The story was told in the 1920s of an old woman, then living in London Row, who was known as a witch. She turned herself into a white hare and ran about the village street at night when the moon was full. One day Farmer Lovelace splashed her with mud when he rode through a gate out hunting. She cursed him and overlooked his cart horses which were found dead in East Farm stables next day.

'The Witch of Piddlehinton' was the subject chosen for a musical, researched and written by Ione Banner. It was performed by the Brownies as the first item on the programme of the 'Evening of Village Entertainment'. This took place in the village hall, the night before the opening of the historical exhibition, 'The Story of Piddlehinton' in March 1988. The legend lives on.